INSTRUCTOR AND STUDENT EDITION

The First-Year College Experience Handbook

Strategies for Academic Success and Character Development

t. leon williams

melissa n. jordan

Copyright © 2014 T. Leon Williams, Melissa N. Jordan
All rights reserved.

ISBN: 1499724772
ISBN 13: 9781499724776
Library of Congress Control Number: 2014910218
CreateSpace Independent Publishing Platform
North Charleston, South Carolina

Preface to Students, Faculty, and Staff

We would like to express our sincere appreciation to you, the students, faculty, and staff of Ohio Northern University, Buena Vista University, and Elon University for affording us the opportunity to learn with you. With more than 20 years of engagement, "Strategies for Academic and Social Success," has instructed, mentored, advised, and coached students towards academic success. Your dedication to this initiative has not gone unnoticed.

The admiration and respect we have for every first-year student is limitless. We value the lived experiences of first-year students as the single most important aspect of college life. Your willingness to embrace this initiative with excitement is the sole reason why we are publishing this work.

We are extremely grateful for the feedback from students and advisors who have used this curriculum to create an environment conducive to the centrality of teaching and learning. Moreover, we applaud those who took advantage of the knowledge and skills this program has to offer.

Foreword to the Instructor and Students
The Practitioners: T. Leon Williams and Melissa Jordan

We have a combined 30 years of student affairs experience. As practitioners, we take great pride in developing student retention programs grounded in research with a proven a record of success. In our experience, we have defined four significant areas of development that help first-year students gain the knowledge and skills needed to matriculate through graduation.

Relationships. Every first-year student needs to secure relationships with students, faculty, staff, alumni, and community members to meet the rigorous academic demands of college.

Academic Readiness. Arguably, the most overlooked aspect of learning is college preparedness. College students today enter into college with varying degrees of academic readiness. All first-year students need to take the necessary steps to ease the transition from high school to college.

Academic and Social Reflection. Often times, students overlook the power of reflecting on the learning experience while they are constantly learning. Every student should acknowledge his or her growth and development through curricular and co-curricular programming.

Transformational Knowledge. For many students, transformational knowledge is integrative knowledge that draws from previous experiences and inserts itself in experiences to come. Transformational knowledge warrants a level of consciousness many first-year students overlook.

First-Year Students

To Students: We wish you the very best as you embark on this living-learning journey. In our experience, first-year students are the single most important resource on campus. You are vibrant and have a high level of curiosity. Every year, first-year students teach us new ways to reach academic and social goals, and in doing so, we have discovered new methods and strategies to ease the transition from high school to college.

Most faculty and staff familiar with this work are envious because their college years did not include such a comprehensive, timely, and resourceful tool. We respect the first-year experience with high-regard, and this guide is your tool to use to make the most of your college experience.

As practitioners, our intent is to uphold two fundamental qualities in our work:

- Your <u>attitude</u> is the key to your success.
- Your <u>approach</u> is the road to your success.

Guidelines for High School Parent/Guardian

If you are parenting a rising junior or senior in high school, we encourage you to utilize this handbook to complement the services already being rendered to your student. In this handbook, you are the Co-Curricular Advisor (CCA). Despite your student(s) learning style or level, this handbook is practical and student-friendly. Look inside and you will find the instructions useful to strengthen your role as Co-Curricular Advisor. *Please remember that you are a partner in your student's learning experience, so take an active role today! We are excited to have you on board as a partner.*

Acknowledgements

Although this texts' primary authorship comes from two learners, it represents the lived experience and expertise from many others. We would be remiss if we failed to acknowledge the scholarly contributions first-year students have holistically enjoyed.

Rationale and Theoretical Framework: Vincent Tinto.
Chapter 2 Stephen R. Covey
Chapter 4 John H. Flavell
Chapter 7 Robert Nash
Chapter 8 Marcia B. Baxter Magolda, Elizabeth G. Creamer, and Peggy S. Meszaros
Chapter 9 Edward T. Hall
Chapter 13 Claude M. Steele
Chapter 14 Elizabeth F. Barkley
Chapter 15 James A. Anderson

Special Acknowledgement to John N. Gardner for his leadership in helping practitioners better understand the experience of first-year college students.

Dedication

First, I would like to dedicate this work to my lifelong partner and best friend, Rochelle and our children, Sierra and Elijah. Thank you for your hugs and kisses. Thank you for understanding the level of commitment warranted to write, volunteer, and mentor. Thank you for allowing me to use my gifts to serve students. This book is also dedicated to my two older children, DeVante and Courtney. I realize now that the miles between us are only pathways towards a greater love. I thank God for you and your prayers, patience, and support.

To my parents, Leroy and Nettie Williams, my brothers, Ivan (LaTonya) and El Jay (Shari), and sister Tenika: I dedicate this work to you. Thank you from the bottom of my heart for teaching me how to laugh, smile, compete, succeed, apologize, and forgive. To my In-laws, Gordon and Sanders families, thank you for supporting the life mission that God has placed on my life.

I would also like to dedicate this work to the Williams family of Youngstown, Ohio, including the Lane, Winford, Tate, Diggs, Robinson, and Harris families. I love you! You are the treasure chest that I draw my energy, passion, drive, and will to survive. A special dedication to my Granny, Deborah Williams, for being who you are: a simply beautiful jewel!

Finally, I dedicate this work to my Co-Author, Melissa Jordan, who serves as a candlelight of peace and love for all. Thank you for your many contributions to this work. Many blessings to you and your family.

Inspiration

This work was initially inspired in 1993. While serving as an Assistant Football Coach at Ohio Northern University, under the leadership of Head Coach Tom Kaczkowski, I was assigned to monitor the study table for student athletes. Thank you Coach Kacz for challenging me to create methods and strategies to increase the retention of student athletes. I thank God for this opportunity.

Brief Note from the Authors

None of this was possible without students! We would like to formally express our sincere appreciation to students from Ohio Northern University in Ada, Ohio (1992 – 2000), Buena Vista University in Storm Lake, Iowa (2000 – 2008), and Elon University in Elon, North Carolina (2008 – 2014). By willingly allowing us to guide your learning, you have been a tremendous help in developing this text. Special thanks to first-year college students for trusting in our partnership.

Like many Student Affairs' professionals, if we started recognizing students, we would certainly leave some out, so we have elected instead to highlight some unique programs that have embraced our curriculum. Special thanks to Ohio Northern University's Black Student Union (BSU), Latina/o Student Union (LSU), Gospel Choir, and Varsity Football team. We would also like to thank Buena Vista University's Students of Diverse Populations, including African-African American Student Union (AASU), Asian American/Pacific Islander (AAPIA), Danse du Coeur, International Club (IC), Multicultural Club (MCC), RAICES, Souldahs, West African Dance, Women of Color (WOC), TimeOut (TO), and Voices of Praise (VOP). Finally, we would like to thank Elon University's Student Mentors Advising Rising Talent (SMART), Watson and Odyssey, National Pan-Hellenic Council, Inc. (NPHC), Diversity Emerging Education Program (DEEP), Men of Character (MOC), and Academic Enrichment Program (AEP).

We thank our families for their unconditional love and support. Many thanks to Leroy and Nettie Williams of Youngstown, Ohio and Delores Jordan and Shawn Jordan (brother) of Camp Springs, MD.

Finally, we thank our mentors: Rev. Dr. Larry E. Covington, Rev. Dr. M. Keith McDaniel, Lenora Billings-Harris, Maria Erb, Dr. Cherrel Miller-Dyce, Anne Wright, Nicole Kleespies, Rev. Ken Meissner, Tom Kaczkowski, Dr. Howard Ward, Mike Jones, Ivan Williams, El-Jay Williams, Tenika Williams, Dr. Kevin Harris, and Jason Reynolds.

Charitable Contribution:
A percentage of your purchase will be dedicated to Kids Read Inc., a nonprofit organization committed to promoting childhood literacy. For more information, please contact Brenna Humphries, Founder, via email kidsreadinc@gmail.com or visit www.kids-read.org.

* * *

The T. Leon Williams Institute for Academic Success and Character Education, LLC (iACE) greatly appreciates your support. To learn more about the institute, please feel free to visit our website: www.leoncharacteredu.com or email: leoncharacter.edu@gmail.com.

RATIONALE AND THEORETICAL FRAMEWORK

Rationale for Academic Excellence:
- Why Was the Program Created?
- Who Will Serve as Co-Curricular Advisors?
- How Often Will Students Meet with Their Co-Curricular Advisor?
- What Does This Mean for Your Campus Climate?

The First-Year Experience
- How Will This Connection Be Made?
- How Will the Co-Curricular Advisors Interact with the First-Year Student?
- Terminology: Students of Diverse Populations
- Theoretical Framework
- Benefits of Intrusive Advising

Five Conditions for Successful Student Retention
- Expectations
- Support
- Feedback
- Involvement
- Relevant Learning

Academic Enrichment with Co-Curricular Advisors and Student Advocates
- Rationale
- Role of Co-Curricular Advisors/Parents
- Role of Student Advocate (Mentor)
- Beneficiaries
- Student Advocate Visual Structure and Pairing Process
- Co-Curricular Advisor Profile
- Student Advocates
    - Student Advocate Overview
    - Student Advocate Mentor philosophy
    - More about the Character Development Curriculum
    - Student Advocate Profile
    - Student Advocate Cluster Groups
    - Brief Note on Student Advocate Training Curriculum

Co-Curricular Advisor and Student Advocate Training Curriculum

Why Was the Program Created?

Student development research consistently informs us that students learn best by doing. Students who are involved in co-curricular experiences are more likely to persist in their education; get better grades; become connected to their peers, faculty and staff, and the university in general; and feel more satisfied with their educational experience. This same research is quick to point out, however, the quality of these co-curricular experiences is relevant and essential if students are to experience these positive results. Thus, random involvement is not as effective as intentional involvement (Upcraft, Gardner & Associates, 1989). Involvement must be meaningful and appropriate; students should be neither under-involved (lack of participation in any co-curricular experience or in activities and organizations that mean little to them and are not directly connected with their academic/career pursuits or personal interests) nor over-extended (involved in too many activities causing them to lose focus, to neglect their academic responsibilities, or feel as though they "do nothing well").

The goal of **Strategies for Academic and Social Success** is to help students make wise and meaningful choices about their co-curricular involvement, which is paramount to their academic success. This handbook exists to inform students about the opportunities available to them, to assist them in linking their personal, academic, and career goals to their co-curricular participation and to help students assess their involvement and how that involvement contributes to their success and/or satisfaction.

Who Will Serve as Co-Curricular Advisors?
Selected members of the faculty and staff team serve in this role. We recommend all participants attend an orientation to discuss the importance of the program and examine roles of the Co-Curricular Advisor. We also recommend Co-Curricular Advisors participate in on-going workshops to help ensure the effectiveness and success of the program. Topics may include advising strategies, mentoring, and/or bias training.

How Often Will Students Meet with Their Co-Curricular Advisor?
The recommended meeting times for Co-Curricular Advisors and students vary from initiative to initiative. At the very least, we recommend Co-Curricular Advisors meet with their advisees once a week for 30 minutes throughout the duration of the semester. The first year of college is the most important year for early success in retention. With this in mind, it is our hope that all Co-Curricular Advisors consider extending their appointment for a second consecutive term. We recommend coffee, tea, breakfast, lunch, or attending workshops, seminars, and keynote addresses together.

What Does This Mean for Your Campus Climate?
Many colleges and universities pride themselves on creating opportunities for engaged learning and leadership. This co-curricular advising initiative is no exception. Research in the field of student affairs has demonstrated little knowledge to similar or related programs. While research supports meaningful and credible involvement in the co-curricular program, the literature in student affairs does not provide information on formal co-curricular advising programs. We are pleased to serve as one of the pioneers in this area and to learn from each other—and our students—as we continue to strengthen this initiative. Most significantly, we see this program as an important service to first-year students, an opportunity for us to help them be more purposeful about their activities and involvement. In turn, we are hopeful that this program will result in your students' greater satisfaction with their educational experience; noted success in attaining academic, career, and personal goals; and, a stronger connection with peers, faculty, staff, and the community at-large.

The First-Year Experience

How Will This Connection Be Made?
We recommend students serve in their cohort as the first point of contact. This may include their first-year seminar cohort, sports team, emerging leaders' cohort, affinity group, or fellows program. Small cohorts serve as a great resource for students transitioning to the academic rigor found in college classrooms.

We also promote with strong conviction the role of the Co-Curricular advisor. After identifying faculty and staff who are committed to the program, each freshman will be assigned a Co-Curricular advisor. We will make every attempt to 'connect' individuals who have had similar personal experiences, and/or we will seek to develop partnerships between those individuals whose strengths are complementary.

How Will the Co-Curricular Advisors Interact with the First-Year Student?
The interaction between the co-curricular advising program and each first-year student is dependent on the needs of the student. At the very least, we hope you will encourage your First-Year Student to take advantage of the programs and services campus-wide, especially those initiatives that support first-year students. We support and highly value ways in which the Co-Curricular Advisors might work collaboratively to develop goals and objectives of the year. The Co-Curricular Advisor can also serve as a resource/link to other student life staff members; thus, if your student has questions or concerns about a certain issue, you can assist in arranging for the staff member to visit with the student. We view this program as a critical service for our students, and also one that, we hope, will assist you in your role as a Co-Curricular Advisor.

Terminology: Students of Diverse Populations
For the purpose of this document, the phrase students of diverse populations will refer to several individuals and groups: students who are a) ethnic minorities, b) academically disadvantaged, c) disabled, d) low socioeconomic status, e) on probation, f) marginalized, g) under-served, and h) gay, lesbian, transgender, and bisexual.

Theoretical Framework
The Co-Curricular Advisor program is based on the theoretical framework of Intrusive Advising. According to Glennan and Baxley (1985), advisors do not wait for students to come forward to ask for help but insist students take an active role in their learning, identify crisis situations, and check on their academic progress routinely. Similarly, Earl (1987) asserted the intrusive model of advising is action-oriented involving qualities of prescriptive advising (expertise, awareness of student needs, structured programs) and of developmental advising (relationship to a student's total needs). The intrusive model of advising promotes strong orientation initiatives, early intervention and outsourcing, and customized academic advising (Earl, 1987).

Effective advisors must insist upon regular contact with their advisees regardless of whether or not assistance is needed (Upcraft & Kramer, 1995). The intrusive model of advising acts as an empowerment tool for students to gain the knowledge and skills to prevent potential problems and take ownership of their learning experience.

Benefits of Intrusive Advising
Intrusive Advising will provide students with the following (Earl, 1987):
- Direct contact with an advisor who deals candidly with the student's academic situation.
- Control over student's own academic structure within the parameters of self-motivation.
- Structured advising programs, which are enhanced by a students' involvement in contract modules.

FIVE CONDITIONS FOR SUCCESSFUL STUDENT RETENTION (Tinto, V. 2000)

EXPECTATIONS
According to Tinto (2000), students are more likely to persist and graduate in settings that clearly define expectations for curricular and co-curricular achievement. As a Co-Curricular Advisor, you are responsible for attending all monthly TEAM MEETINGS. Team Meetings are meetings with advisors and multicultural staff. You are expected to meet with your advisees weekly or biweekly, if applicable. You are expected to follow the program as outlined in the Academic Enrichment Program and SMART manuals.

SUPPORT
"Support" for students of diverse populations has been defined in myriad of ways (i.e., tutoring, study groups, academic support, counseling, mentoring, and ethnic student centers). For the purpose of this document, we are defining "support" as consistent contact with advisees. Co-Curricular Advisors who understand the importance of steady communication in minimizing the challenges students of diverse populations face are in the best position to assist students in making quality academic and social decisions (Heisserer, Parette, 2002). Your support is vital to the overall progress of the student. Tinto found that academic support is most effective when it is connected to the students' daily living and learning (2000).

FEEDBACK
We invite you to provide feedback on an ongoing basis to the Multicultural Center staff. We will provide each advisor with a formal assessment instrument to monitor the growth and development of each advisee. All advisors will be asked to complete end of the semester evaluations. We also hope you will tell us of ideas you have regarding how to improve the program as the semester progresses. Research shows students are more likely to succeed in college settings that provide frequent and substantial feedback (Tinto, 2000).

INVOLVEMENT
Unlike any other advising program, the Co-Curricular Advisor program warrants the leadership and expertise of highly engaged faculty and staff. This means you are the qualified, caring faculty and/or staff member responsible for advocating healthy living, wellness, good decision-making, good judgment, and processing. Tinto (2000) points out that students who are academically and socially involved are more likely to matriculate to graduation. Your notice and encouragement of student involvement is essential to students' continued success in the classroom.

RELEVANT LEARNING
As members of the education community, we value curricular and co-curricular experiences as "relevant learning" experiences. Personal experiences are also relevant learning experiences. Tinto (2000) says the more student find value in their learning, the more they see their experience connected to their interests, which is paramount to learning and perseverance. Advisors are responsible for helping students make new meaning in curricular and co-curricular experiences.

Academic Enrichment with Co-Curricular Advisors and Student Advocates

Strategies for Academic and Social Success are geared towards, but not limited to, first-year students. There are no academic requirements to implement this program. This program challenges students to take authority over their academic and social experience. Students in the program will be responsible for completing a 15-week academic and social strategies curriculum. We highly recommend students participate in a peer mentoring or cohort program. We have seen students achieve the greatest success in these types of peer-to-peer programs. *More information regarding mentoring will be discussed later in the handbook.*

Rationale: In our experience and study, combined academic and social development programs provide first-year students, diverse populations, and first-generation students with the greatest opportunities for success. Marrying the academic and social lives of students in an advising role creates a *holistic* approach that addresses the two major concerns for these populations: academic performance and social integration into campus life (Engle & Tinto, 2008). Co-curricular advisors are critical to student retention as our student population is less likely to make connections with faculty and staff and therefore has less support and knowledge of how to navigate the bureaucratic aspects of academic and social life in college (Engle & Tinto, 2008; Astin, 1997).

Role of Co-Curricular/Parent Advisors: Co-Curricular advisors take an "active and intrusive" approach to advising in order to meet the needs of our diverse student population. This approach requires Co-Curricular Advisors to meet frequently with mentees to create a check point and safety net for students and to track students' academic and social progress (Engle & Tinto, 2008). Co-Curricular Advisors must provide personalized attention, services, and referrals; they serve as first-responders to students' needs and concerns (Engle & Tinto, 2008). This "active and intrusive approach" to advising provides first-year students with the necessary resources and skills to be successful in their first year of college and beyond.

Role of the Student Advocate (Mentor): The Student Advocate serves in a unique role by offering a different level of empathy and support from their firsthand student experience. The Student Advocate is trained to address non-academic stressors that directly connect to academic performance, such as social development and a sense of belonging in a new community (Rosenthal & Shinebarger, 2010). For many students of diverse populations, entering a new environment creates issues of marginality and mattering. First-year students desire to develop a feeling of fitting in and mattering to those around them (Evans, Forney & Guido-DiBrito, 1998). The Student Advocate addresses these and other issues through face-to-face interactions, guided discussions, and by planning of experiences shared by the cohort/mentee group and Co-Curricular Advisors. This small social network provides an intentional and intimate group that will fill a pivotal role in first-year students' transition and matriculation.

Beneficiaries:
- Academic Advising
- Community College
- College Mentor Programs
- Diversity and Inclusion
- First-year Experience programs
- Graduating High School Seniors
- Military students
- Nontraditional Students
- Parents
- Student Affairs

Student Advocate Visual Structure and Pairing Process:

First-year students will be intentionally paired with a Student Advocate and a Co-Curricular Advisor based on their academic and social interests. The primary role of the Student Advocate is to facilitate the Character Development conversations, which are highlighted at the beginning of each chapter. It is important to note here that we are not meaning to suggest the Student Advocate needs to be present during the Co-Curricular Advisor and First-Year Student meetings. The Student Advocate will meet separately with the First-Year Student(s) (i.e., for lunch, at the library, or residence hall, for coffee/tea, etc.). We recommend one (1) Student Advocate per Co-Curricular Advisor and First-Year Student pairing. Below is a diagram that displays the integration of the Student Advocate and the Co-Curricular Advisor.

Key
CCA: Co-Curricular Advisor
SA: Student Advocate
FYS: First-Year Student

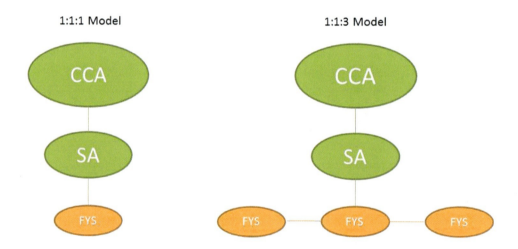

In the event that you decide to use the cohort model, we recommend the 1:1:3 model, which involves a Co-Curricular Advisor, a Student Advocate, and three first-year students. We recommend that the cohort not exceed three first-year students. We strongly advise against assigning more than three first-year students to a Student Advocate. Please keep in mind that the Student Advocate is also striving for his or her own academic and social success.

Co-Curricular Advisors' Expectations

We have seen the best results from this program in situations where the expectations are clear and concise. With this in mind, every Co-Curricular Advisor is expected to receive training before engaging with students. This manual will serve as a guide for the discussion. We recommend you utilize the social development discussion topics below to guide the conversation. We also recommend you take advantage of the expertise on your campus.

You will notice the Student Advocate is asked to facilitate a similar conversation. Our intent is not to be repetitive. Instead, our goal is to surround first-year students with the support and advocacy they need to be successful. We value the shared perspective of students, faculty, and staff.

In our practice, we have noticed the way in which students hold Student Advocate and Co-Curricular Advisor conversations in high-regard. Moreover, our experience tells us that students persevere to graduation at a much higher rate when they have Student Advocate and Co-Curricular Advisor support than their peers who do not have the same support.

We draw twelve core competencies for Co-Curricular Advisors from our experience. For the best results, we recommend all Co-Curricular Advisor demonstrate competency in the following areas:
- Intellectual Curiosity
- Transition to College
- Personality Conflicts and Group Dynamics
- Conflict Resolution
- Social Networking
- Goal Setting
- Social Capital
- Physical and Mental Health Awareness
- Identity Formation
- Alienation and Homesickness
- Bias Education
- Power and Privilege

Time and Commitment to Students

We strongly advocate for one-on-one meetings. These meetings are designed so as not to exceed 60 minutes. It is important to note that the time allotted is not set in stone. We recommend you allow some flexibility in the schedule for unplanned circumstances. Similarly, we recognize that students learn in various ways, and some students grasp concepts and ideas with very little supervision or coaching.

In the event that you decide to implement the program to a cohort group, we recommend that the meeting run between two and three hours. Please remember: you should employ a Student Advocate for every three first-year students. The same goals can be achieved in both the cohort group setting and the one-on-one meetings. We have seen great results with both approaches to this work.

Co-Curricular Advisor Profile

Below are suggestions to consider when recruiting faculty, staff, and support staff to become Co-Curricular Advisors. It is important that there is a diverse pool of Co-Curricular Advisors. We highly recommend that you send an "all-call" campus-wide email for volunteers to serve as Co-Curricular Advisors, and select individuals who best fit the profile of your students (major, minor, geographical location, commuter, etc.) We recommend seeking diversity in all of the following categories as a baseline for attracting Co-Curricular Advisors:

Gender
Race
Ethnicity
Religion
Department
Teaching
Research

Student Advocates

Student Advocate Overview: What is a Student Advocate?

The Student Advocate is a peer mentor who serves as a liaison between the First-Year Student and Co-Curricular Advisor. The Student Advocate was introduced to the program in 2006 as an added layer of support to first-year students. The primary task of the Student Advocate was to serve as a resource of information to help students navigate the first-year experience. Today, the Student Advocate is charged with the task of fusing the social development curriculum and the academic experience. Student Advocates are highly skilled in the first-year experience. The skilled knowledge of using their personal narrative to empower and orient first-year students to campus is what separates the Student Advocate from other campus mentors.

Student Advocates are sophomore, junior, and senior students who are trained to provide support and guidance to first-year students and to ensure students engage in a successful transition to college. Student Advocates serve as a first-responder to student academic and social needs. The Student Advocate understands the multiple factors that affect learning, including the learning environment. The Student Advocate helps students make meaning of their classroom and co-curricular experiences.

To be a Student Advocate, we recommend each student participate in peer-to-peer training. In our experience, we have seen peer-to-peer mentoring as one of the most influential methods of increasing first-year student retention and persistence to graduation rates.

Student Advocate Mentoring Philosophy

The Student Advocate Philosophy is to listen, serve, and follow up. The Student Advocate understands his/her unique role in supporting first-year students in the wake of their academic pursuits. The Student Advocate is trained to serve as a sounding board for student highlights and concerns. The Student Advocate is committed to providing leadership in conversations related to academic excellence and social networking. Finally, the Student Advocate understands the importance of making meaningful and lasting relationships with clear expectations and communication.

More about the Character Development Curriculum

Each Character Development conversation is designed to invite first-year students to reflect on their academic and social experience. This conversation provides the First-Year Student and Student Advocate with the opportunity to navigate systems and structures, plan-ahead, and problem-solve. Moreover, each conversation is designed to develop a course of action for implementation. More importantly, each Character Development conversation is designed to complement the Co-Curricular Advisor conversation, as noted above.

When a Student Advocate approaches the Character Development conversation in this way, it is the Student Advocate's questioning and reflection skills that deepen the First-Year-Student's thinking processes. Ultimately, it is our intent that the First-Year Student not become dependent on the Student Advocate but instead become an independent critical thinker. The First-Year Student is encouraged to construct his/her own thinking patterns, which is paramount to the empowerment of self. In the same spirit, the First-Year Student is responsible for his/her actions.

Student Advocate Profile

What should you look for when recruiting students to become Student Advocates? It is important that there is a diverse pool of Student Advocates. In other words, the pool of volunteers must meet the needs of your student(s) or cohort(s). We recommend seeking diversity in all of the following categories as a baseline for attracting Student Advocates:

Gender
Race
Ethnicity
Religion
Year in College
Major
Minor

Other Considerations
Student Athlete?
Greek Letter Organization?
Affinity Group Affiliate?
Student Government Representative?
Able-bodied?
Residence Life?

Student Advocate Cluster Groups

The purpose of the Student Advocate Cluster Groups is to provide Student Advocates with additional support in the form of accountability partners for their work with first-year students. A "Cluster" here is being defined as a pair of Student Advocates. The purpose of the cluster is to help the Student Advocate address untimely, uncontrollable circumstances. Examples of untimely and uncontrollable circumstances may include gender preferences, major differentiation, sexual orientation, or geographical support. We are not suggesting making changes to an established cohort is necessary when these circumstances arise, but additional Student Advocate support can also help diversify support of the First-Year Student. The Cluster Group is also helpful when planning social and academic events (i.e., cookouts, study groups, movie nights, or student night-outs). *The Cluster Group does not impact the Co-Curricular Advisor.*

The diagram below may be helpful when organizing your Cluster Groups. This is one example of a Cluster Group. We encourage you to be creative in naming your Cluster: we call this group "Ninja."

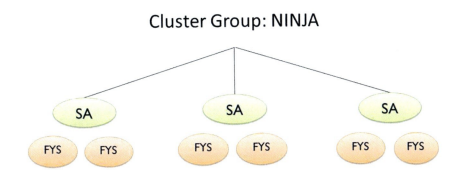

Brief Note on Student Advocate Training Curriculum

Student Advocate Training is the single most important aspect of the peer coach leadership position. First-year students reported that their Student Advocates were the most influential voices in regards to their academic and social development. With this in mind, we recommend Student Advocates devote one week to training. We recommend Student Advocates meet in the Spring, Summer, or Fall, depending on availability. The training can also be condensed into a two or three day orientation held prior to opening weekend.

Throughout the training sessions, Student Advocates will grapple with topics such as limitations and boundaries, healthy and unhealthy relationships, support versus advocacy, personal growth and development, biases and misconceptions, and how to live a balanced lifestyle. Most importantly, the Student Advocate will receive extensive training on campus resources. It is very important that the Student Advocate is fully aware of the academic and social support services rendered to students.

Other training discussions must include crisis intervention and bias response education. We suggest that your Student Advocate join Residence Life, Multicultural/Diversity Affairs, or Bias Response Team, to learn more about best practices in addressing crisis and acts of bias. Training related to these areas of development has proven beneficial to the Student Advocate and first-year student relationship.

Supplemental material that can be used for training to manage and resolve conflict include Strengths Quest inventory, SWOT analysis, Myers-Briggs Type Indicator, Strong Interest Inventory, among others. Ultimately, we want Student Advocates to understand the seriousness of their role as the number one social resource.

Additionally, we recommend utilizing campus resources to facilitate difficult dialogues in the training. Resources may include: Bias Response Team, Multicultural Affairs, Religious Life, Career Services, Judicial, Residence Life, Counseling, Health and Well-being, Academic Affairs, Leadership, and Greek life, among others. These types of resources have proven advantageous to Student Advocates and First-Year Students.

Co-Curricular Advisor and Student Advocate Training Curriculum

For the purpose of this handbook, we have decided to provide an outline for the training curriculum. This outline can be used for Student Advocate and Co-Curricular Advisor training. It is our intent to create a seamless and enriching training curriculum to train Student Advocates and Co-Curricular Advisors to assist First-Year Students in leading and authoring academic and social transitions to college. Please feel free to modify this outline to meet the needs of your campus.

CURRICULUM TRAINING OUTLINE

I. **Understanding the Strategies for Academic and Social Success.** Please review the handbook thoroughly. It is important that you become familiar with the methods and strategies of this handbook to effectively facilitate conversations and provide students with the most informed suggestions.

II. **Understanding the Academic Curriculum.** Become familiar with your institution's academic culture, including semester breaks, mid-term and final exams, advising, and registering for subsequent semesters.

III. **Understanding the purpose of one-on-one meetings.** The 1:1 meetings are designed to bridge the gap between you and the First-Year Student. This time is about helping the students navigate their college career.

IV. **Understanding the cohort philosophy.** If you plan to utilize the cohort model, it is a must that you have very informed discussions with the First-Year Student, Student Advocates, and Co-Curricular Advisors. The cohort model is our effort to cast a wide net. Make certain that every student receives the attention he or she deserves. The integrity of the curriculum must not be compromised.

V. **Knowing limitations and boundaries.** If and when conversations with first-year students move beyond your comfort or expertise, please be aware of your limitations and boundaries. Ignoring these signs could have an adverse effect on students.

VI. **Knowing Campus Resources.** Depending on the culture of your campus, it may be important to generate a list of faculty, staff, and support staff who will be available to support your efforts. For many reasons (including gender, race, religion, etc), it may be best to have this list accessible to Co-Curricular Advisors and Student Advocates.

VII. **The Importance of Academic Honesty and Integrity.** Become familiar with the academic policies at your institution. Clear and concise expectations are essential to your ability to help students equip themselves with the knowledge to uphold the academic integrity of the institution.

VIII. **Self-Assessment.** Are you prepared to engage in these conversations? It is important to assess your other time commitments and level of commitment to the program before volunteering in this role.

IX. **Early Alerts, Warnings, and Cautions.** Become familiar with the physical and emotional trends of first-year students in their first semester in college. Pay close attention to the ethos of the academic and social calendar.

X. **Diversity Education.** *It is of the utmost importance that the Student Advocate and Co-Curricular Advisor assess their biases, preconceived notions, and misconceptions prior to meeting with students.*

Student Population Served

The role of the Co-Curricular Advisor is just as important as, if not more important than, that of the peer mentor. The availability of ideal, caring role models/mentors is valuable for all students, but may be especially critical to the retention and success of underrepresented, first-generation college students who do not have college role models at home (Lee, 1999). Vince Tinto (1987) says, "While role modeling seems to be effective in retention programs generally, it appears to be especially important among those programs concerned with disadvantaged [underrepresented] students" (p.161). It has become increasingly important to provide our diverse students with a high level of support for advisors and peers. The intrusive advising model is most important in encouraging the success of our students.

Trained to support the needs for our students of diverse populations, Student Advocates work primarily with, but not only with, students who identify as racially/ethnically diverse, first-generation, LGBTQ, and/or have low socioeconomic status. With this in mind, it is important for advisors to be aware of the specific needs affecting these diverse populations of students. According to research conducted on college campuses nationwide, students of diverse populations often experience psychological stressors and feelings of alienation, loneliness, lack of social integration, and lack of support at white-majority institutions (Guiffrida & Douthit 2010). For many of these students, intentional support from peers and advisors is critical for their matriculation to graduation and success in their academic career. For each student, college experiences can be categorized into academic experiences and social experiences (Tinto, 1987). It is imperative for the Co-Curricular Advisor to ensure that these students are developing a healthy lifestyle in and outside of the classroom. It is also important for students to be able to identify resources, and, more importantly, role models, to assist them in their transition to college.

Taking this notion one step further, it is essential for each Co-Curricular Advisor to be mindful of the cultural implications of learning in a seemingly adverse environment. Within the student experience, there may be significant conflict between the student's culture and the institutions culture (Lee, 1999). Differences in cultural identity and cultural capital may be hurdles the student will need to tackle in his/her pursuit of academic success. In an effort to best support students of diverse populations, each Co-Curricular Advisor will be responsible for researching best practices for retaining students of diverse populations at white-majority institutions. It is important to note here that, as we have found in our practice that white students face similar challenges to those faced by historically marginalized individuals and groups. Many of the "-isms" (racism, classism, sexism, and other discriminatory philosophies of thought) may play into each student experience in the campus culture. The role of the Co-Curricular Advisor, in this manner, is one of support and empowerment. Students need to feel they have an advisor with whom they have developed a trusting relationship and who will support and empower them as they shape and develop their experience during their first-year transition.

As an advisor, you will meet with each student for 30-60 minutes weekly to discuss academic progress and social engagement. During this time, topics of social engagement and development will include topics specific to the student experience outside of the classroom. ***It is up to the discretion of the advisor to judge the most important ways to utilize the 30-60 minute time slot.*** Along with this guide, we recommend you develop a resource list that all advisors can utilize to become familiar with specific issues that affect the diverse student population on a white-majority campus. A student's success is attributed to the combination of classroom experiences and out-of-classroom experiences. The time spent and work completed between the Co-Curricular Advisor and the student is essential to the overall development and success of the student.

Academic Integrity

Underlining this curriculum is the idea of Academic Integrity. We cannot assume every student, faculty member, and staff member thoroughly understands the significance of Academic Integrity, so we have taken this opportunity to mention its importance. In our view, Academic Integrity is not solely a classroom policy; Academic Integrity is each student's personal responsibility as he or she creates an environment that recognizes and affirms the uniqueness of each student to create a vibrant learning environment for all.

We recognize every institution may define Academic Integrity differently, but we have found that students, faculty, and staff increase their day-to-day interactions when the learning and living environment is welcoming and supportive. As a valued member of your learning environment, you have the responsibility to uphold Academic Integrity at the highest level of academic excellence.

The core values below represent how students, faculty, and staff must be partners in learning. It is our intent to close the gap between the scholar and the student. These core values are essential to forming new relationships in diverse settings. This understanding is the thread that binds the Co-Curricular Advisor, Student Advocate, and First-Year Student relationship.

※ ※ ※

Core Values

AUTHENTICITY: Be genuine.

HONORABLITY: Be truthful.

DEPENDABILITY: Be responsible.

HUMILITY: Be respectful.

BENEFITS:
- Transparency
- Open-mindedness
- Clear communications
- Clear expectations
- Breadth and Depth

Contents

Part 1 Relationships 1

Introduction Week: Introduction to Academic and Social Success 2
    Character Development: Laying the Foundation for Academic and Social Success ... 3
    Academic Development: Self-Image Checklist 4
    Academic Development: Consent Form 6
    Academic Development: Student Profile Form 8
    Academic Development: Introduction Letter 10
    Academic Development: Learning Committee 11
    Communication Log Sheets 12

Chapter 1 The Co-Curricular Advisor & Student Relationship 15
    Character Development: Identifying the Best YOU! 16
    Academic Development: Value Inventory 17
    Academic Development: Energy Line 19
    Academic Development: Energy Line 20
    Academic Development: Personal Contract 21

Chapter 2 Getting Adjusted & Planning for Academic Success 22
    Character Development: Around the Clock Personal Development and Self-Care ... 23
    Academic Development: Academic Playbook: 1st and 10 24
    Academic Development: Academic Spaces 26
    Academic Development: Time Pie 28
    Academic Development: Time-Wasters 30
    Academic Development: Time Management 31
    Academic Development: Time Management Matrix 33

Chapter 3 Academic and Social Peaks and Valleys 35
    Character Development: The Blueprint for Managing Goals 36
    Academic Development: Academic Goals 39
    Academic Development: Personal Asset Mapping 41

Part 2 Academic Readiness 43

Chapter 4 Unveil Your Brain Power & Discover the Learner in You 44
    Character Development: Thinking About Thinking 45
    Academic Development: Metacognition 46

Chapter 5 Strategies for Success & Valuing the Learning Experience 49
    Character Development: Choosing to Learn to Succeed 50
    Academic Development: Personal Value Assessment 51

  Academic Development: Reading the Environment 53
  Academic Development: Mind Mapping. 55

Chapter 6 Mid-term Prep & Meaningful Experiences and Relationships 57
  Character Development: Academic Road Trip 58
  Academic Development: Mid-term Preparation 60
  Academic Development: Transferrable Skills. 63

Part 3: Academic and Social Reflection 65

Chapter 7 Crucial Conversations in Diverse Settings 66
  Character Development: Deepening the Significance of Learning 67
  Academic Development: Meaning-Making 68

Chapter 8 Applied Engaged Learning 69
  Character Development: Rewriting the Headlines 70
  Academic Development: Student Intelligence and Self-Authorship. 72
  Academic Development: Engaged Learning Differences. 74

Chapter 9 Assessing the "Living-Learning" Experience. 75
  Character Development: It Takes a Village 76
  Academic Development: Meaningful Relationships 77

Chapter 10 New Environments Call for New Perspectives 79
  Character Development: Journey Walk 80
  Academic Development: Academic Wellness. 81

Chapter 11 Do More by Doing Less. 84
  Character Development: Emulating Success 85
  Academic Development: Efficiency and Effectiveness. 87

Part 4: Transformative Knowledge 91

Chapter 12 Social Intelligence 92
  Character Development: "A Piece of the Puzzle". 93
  Character Development: Managing the Mask. 95
  Character Development: Social Situational Awareness 96
  Academic Development: Academic Situational Awareness 98

Chapter 13 Bias in the Face of Diversity. 100
  Character Development: Identity Development and Critical Thinking 101
  Academic Development: Transformative Experience. 103
  Academic Development: Stereotype Threat 105

Chapter 14 Intellectual Diversity. 107
        Character Development: Crossing the Finish Line 108
        Academic Development: Erasing Doubt. 109

Chapter 15 Diversity Intelligence Matters. 111
        Character Development: The Significance of Diverse Thinking 112
        Academic Development: Access to Bias. 114
        Academic Development: Diversity Intelligence Rubric. 116

References 119

Author Biography. 123

Character Development Guide and Contents

Co-Curricular Guide Overview

Pep-Talk for Co-Curricular Advisors and Student Advocates

As partners in this program, you will have the opportunity to help students monitor their progress in the classroom, to develop a rapport with their professors at greater depth, and to take authority over their learning. The Strategies for Academic and Social Success Handbook is designed to help students filter the many distractions that influence learning. In addition, the Strategies for Academic and Social Success Handbook will provide students with the ability to develop their own perspectives on learning and to make new meanings out of the learning experience.

Student Learning Outcomes: Students will gain the following:

- Knowledge of strengths and weaknesses
- Critical thinking skills
- Knowledge of the power of self-authorship
- Ability to make decisions about knowledge gained
- Trust in one's own ability to learn
- Confidence to direct one's life as a productive individual
- Knowledge to develop one's own perspective on education and life

The Strategies for Academic and Social Success Handbook is grounded in one fundamental framework: power. According to Hawkins (2002), power can be described as upliftment, dignity, and meaning. Power is total and complete and requires nothing from the outside (Hawkins, 2002). For the betterment of the program, power can be seen as the mental and physical function instilled in you that requires no manipulation to be in existence. Power supplies and supports—it energizes and gives life (Hawkins, 2002).

Within this ideal is the notion of attitude and approach. As a fortress of the curriculum, students' attitude towards learning is the single most important aspect for creating positive outcomes. If you examine and change your attitude toward a learning experience your approach to the classroom experience will change. This curriculum will provide students with a healthy approach to regain the power to navigate through the curriculum.

Unlike some Early Alert structures found in education, Strategies for Academic and Social Success is a proactive approach to learning that challenges students to draw on their strengths and underdevelopments to regain their momentum to be successful. This handbook features strategic objectives designed for academic and social development.

Are You Ready? Let's Do It!

Part 1 Relationships

Ants organize a colony for one common goal: survival. The ant colony is a trustworthy society designed to care for its own. Accountability and dependability are two of the most dominant characteristics of ants. These characteristics help all members of the colony survive.

Like ants, students should form meaningful relationships with other students. They should share one goal: to build relationships that benefit the community. Students should be in sync with one another, unselfishly helping each other achieve maximum success.

INTRODUCTION WEEK

Introduction to Academic and Social Success

"This program was extremely beneficial to our son while attending Elon University. As parents, we worry when our children go off to college and how they will adjust to the many challenges during the transition...because we know there will definitely be some trials. So, one of the biggest questions for us was, *"Who will be there to support and help our son if/when he needs it?"* This academic program answered all of our questions.

The program helped our son adjust academically and socially; and to find a balance that would allow him to excel and reach his full potential. This program is truly an excellent program and we are thankful that Elon embraces the Multicultural Center and all of its programs."

Pam Holmes, Parent of 2014 Graduate

Character Development:
Laying the Foundation for Academic and Social Success

Take a moment to discuss the following character development topics with your student. The objective is to draw a correlation between student values, academic culture, and social development. This is an open discussion. We encourage the Student Advocate and First-Year Student to share personal stories. This exercise will help them to gain knowledge about one another and to use the skill of self-authorship.

- ☐ **The power of critical questions.** The more you ask yourself questions about your transition to college, the more you deepen your understanding of your purpose on campus.

- ☐ **Give yourself permission to try.** This is a very important time in your life. It is quite natural to feel apprehensive. Give yourself a chance to broaden your academic and social perspectives in a positive way.

- ☐ **Challenge yourself to be a conscious student.** With all the excitement and hype of the first week of school, find time to personally reflect on the learning experience you are about to encounter.

- ☐ **Take advantage of all the learning community has to offer.** Explore campus and community resources. Learning can occur in and outside the classroom.

- ☐ **Strengthen who you are by what you do.** Organization is a very important skill for a successful start in college. Be organized in every facet of the first-year experience (including, but not limited to, class, exercise, studying, eating habits, and sleeping).

- ☐ **Know that every opportunity to improve is available to you.** *Knowing* the campus and community resources can help strengthen your ability to succeed in college.

- ☐ **Know your limitations and boundaries.** Too often, first-year students lose sight of the self in the midst of the transition to college. This is the perfect time to assess your limitations and boundaries.

- ☐ **It's never too early to ask for help.** Don't wait until you start feeling the pressures of college to ask for help. You know you better than anyone else does! Know the symptoms of your own anticipated failure (mentally, physically) and seek help before it happens.

- ☐ **Be familiar with your learning style.** If you haven't already done so, explore your learning styles with a faculty member. There are great benefits to knowing why you are excited about some classes and distracted from others.

- ☐ **Learn the learner.** Hone in on your academic and social skills. Learn how to teach and learn from your experiences. Your peers are counting on you to succeed.

- ☐ **Diversify your academic and social portfolio.** Branch out to students of diverse populations. Attend different programs and events on campus.

- ☐ **Be excited about what's next.** Don't rush to solve it all in a day or week. Leave some excitement and mystery for the next turn or adventure on campus or in the community.

INTRODUCTION TO ACADEMIC AND SOCIAL SUCCESS

Academic Development: Self-Image Checklist

<u>Introduction Week Instruction: The CCA & First-Year Student Relationship</u>
In this new relationship, it is important to define the relationship between the Co-Curricular Advisor (CCA) and the student. The role of the Co-Curricular Advisor is to be a resource and advocate for the student. In this opening exercise, the CCA and student will discuss the importance of getting off to a great start. One of the keys to a great college experience is identifying the self. We recommend every first-year student develop a Self-Image checklist to routinely assess his or her progress in the classroom and outside the classroom.
CCA Directions: Review and discuss each area of development with your student.

- **Be on time for class and meetings.**
  It is imperative that all first-year students are on time for class and meetings. If you think you will be late or absent, contact the faculty member or your Co-Curricular Advisor immediately.

- **Be prepared to teach and learn.**
  Nothing is more gratifying than engagement in learning. Be prepared to lead discussion; show that you have read the material, and be prepared to examine the reading at a much greater depth.

- **Have an outline of your schedule.**
  It is in the student's best interest to develop a *plan of action* for meeting the expectations of your course work and co-curricular commitments.

- **Discuss your expectations with your faculty and Co-Curricular Advisor.**
  Every first-year student must develop a set of academic and social expectations to avoid being over involved. Open dialogue allows the faculty and your Co-Curricular Advisor to collaborate in your learning experience. Initiate conversations with them.

- **Don't dismiss your apprehensions.**
  Concerns about your college experience are real. Do not ignore your emotions. By neglecting your emotions, you may increase your stress level.

- **Discuss strengths and weaknesses.**
  At this stage of your development, clear knowledge of your strengths and weaknesses is essential to understanding how you learn best. Knowing how you learn best will be helpful in determining a career path and how best to approach it.

- **Discuss boundaries and limitations.**
  Think about your learning and communication styles, as those often indicate how you engage in dialogue and interact with others effectively. Specifically, ask yourself what factors play a major role in your learning and communication styles. Some examples may include, but are not limited to, language, culture, socio-economic status, and geographical location. These factors can have a positive impact on learning.

- **Identify campus resources.**
  There is a variety of resources on campus that are designed to help students to have a healthy college experience and to pursue academic excellence. Campus resources may include a speaker center, a writing center, and a wellness center.

- **Learn to solve problems.**
  How do you handle conflict? How do you best communicate when disagreement is present? It is important for first-year students to identify the strategies that are most effective for them when addressing difficult dialogues in the classroom.

- **Getting Involved.**
  Participate in the student organization fair, but consider limiting your choices to two to three organizations.

INTRODUCTION TO ACADEMIC AND SOCIAL SUCCESS

Academic Development: Consent Form

Introduction Week Instruction: The CCA & First-Year Student Relationship
CCA Directions: It is important that the CCA and First-Year Student discuss and complete the consent form. The purpose of the consent form is to protect the rights of the student and the CCA. In addition, the Consent Form provides an opportunity to discuss roles. Mentoring and advising is more effective with co-authored expectations.

Purpose: Take advantage of the Strategies for Academic and Social Success to learn more about your progress in the classroom. Hear directly from professors on areas for improvement.

We advise the Co-Curricular Advisors to contact the student's professors and learn more about the student's achievements and challenges in the classroom. The intent of this curriculum is to provide students with feedback to enrich the learning experience. First, ask the student to complete the consent form. Due to high volume of reported cases of violations of student confidentiality, we recommend the CCA take extreme caution in collecting individual student information made available to the CCA by completion this form. The document below is an example of the consent form. Please feel free to modify this form to meet the needs of your institution.

A draft of a student consent form for access to education progress can be found below. This form can be used as a binding agreement between the student and the program administrator. This is an internal document that is not to be shared with the general public. None of the information discussed in this document will be accessed by any other non-acting partner.

THE FIRST-YEAR COLLEGE EXPERIENCE HANDBOOK

INSTITUTION NAME (HERE)

Student Name (Last, First, Middle Initial): _____ Date: _____

The Family Educational Rights and Privacy Act (FERPA) affords certain rights to students concerning the privacy of, and access to, education records. Students may choose to complete and submit this form to the Registrar allowing the release of their education records to specified third parties. Please note that while this form authorizes (Program Name/Professional Staff) to release education records to third parties, it does not obligate (Institution Name) to do so. (Institution Name) reserves the right to review and respond to requests for release of education records on a case-by-case basis. For additional information, please visit the U.S. Department of Education's website at www.ed.gov/policy/gen/guide/fpco/ferpa/index.html.

A. Education records to be released:

___ (Initial) Academic Information (grades/GPA, class, registration, student ID number, enrollment status)

B. Person(s) to whom access to education records may be provided:

_____

Name(s) of person(s) to whom access to records may be provided

_____

Campus Email and Addresses   Relationship to Student

C. Duration of Release (Check One):

☐ **One-Time Use:** This authorization can be used only once.

☐ **Limited Use:** This authorization expires on: _____

D. Purpose of release (Check One):

☐ Family Communication

☐ Employment

☐ Co-Curricular Advising

☐ Program Assessment Administrator

In understand that (1) I have the right to refuse to consent to the release of my education records, (2) I have the right to inspect any written records released in effect of this Consent, and (3) I have the right to revoke this consent at any time by delivering a written revocation to the university's Registrar Office.

_____   _____   _____   _____
Student's Signature   Date   Signature of Parent or Guardian (if under 18)   Date

- *This form must be fully completed and signed by the student. Records cannot be released if any Section of this form is not filled out. Please return this form to the program administrator.*

INTRODUCTION TO ACADEMIC AND SOCIAL SUCCESS

Academic Development: Student Profile Form

Introduction Week Instruction: The CCA & First-Year Student Relationship

CCA Directions: Students should complete this form before their first one-on-one meeting with the Co-Curricular Advisor. Please use this information as a conversation starter with the student to learn more about their living-learning environment and any apprehensions they may have.

THE FIRST-YEAR COLLEGE EXPERIENCE HANDBOOK

Student Profile Form

Student Name: _____ Date: _____

Program/Scholarship: _____

School Address: _____ Cell Phone: _____ Email: _____

Housing Assignment: _____ Roommate: _____

Circle One: Fr   So   Jr   Sr

Reason(s) for joining AEP

[ ] Academic Status   [ ] Motivation   [ ] Social   [ ] Anger

[ ] Absences   [ ] Alcohol   [ ] Drugs   [ ] Financial Planning

[ ] Stress   [ ] Depression   [ ] Time Mgt.   [ ] Study Skills

[ ] Mental Health   [ ] Emotional Health   [ ] Spiritual   [ ] Death

[ ] Other: _____

Academic and Social Concerns: _____
_____
_____
_____
_____

Co-Curricular Advisor's Signature: _____ Date _____
Student Signature: _____ Date _____

After your discussion, please return this form to the program administrator. Program administrator: keep this form in your records for pre- and post-assessment.

INTRODUCTION TO ACADEMIC AND SOCIAL SUCCESS

Academic Development: Introduction Letter

Introduction Week Instruction: The CCA & First-Year Student Relationship

CCA Directions: Students are required to share with their Co-Curricular Advisor a draft of their personal email to their professors. At the doctoral level, candidates are encouraged to contact experts in their field of study to serve on their doctoral committee. The candidate's first step in achieving this goal is to contact the expert directly via introduction letter. This form of communication allows the candidate to share background information, area of study, and concerns.

In the same spirit, we encourage the First-Year Student to introduce his or herself to the faculty. Although unorthodox and challenging, this approach has proven advantageous to students. This approach has provided students with the confidence to communicate with their faculty without any reservations. We have found that today's students are relational. A vast majority of students say having a relationship with faculty and staff is key to their academic and social success.

Examples of subjects to include in the letter: background information, high school, hometown, major, interests, hobbies, scholarships, student involvement, family, employment, mentor(s), advisor(s), anticipated interest in the course, etc.

EXAMPLE

Dear Professor,

I am contacting you to personally introduce myself. I am enrolled in your 9:00 a.m. Marketing class on Tuesday and Thursday. I am excited about the learning opportunity we will share this semester. This semester I am working closely with the _____ (program name) through the Academic Advising Office. My Advisor there is _____, and he/she will be contacting you throughout the semester to check on my progress. Please feel free to contact them as well.

I signed up for your class because I want to learn more about the intricacies of marketing. Moreover, I would like to learn more about [here, talk about your interest in the class, how marketing can strengthen your career aspirations and other career endeavors].

I enjoy challenges [talk about your character and areas of improvement].

As a student, I am involved with [talk about the clubs and organizations, service, employment, volunteerism].

With this in mind, I would like to [talk about any additional support systems].

In closing, [talk about your excitement, concerns, apprehensions, anticipation].

Sincerely,

Ricky Williams, First-Year Student

Academic Development: Learning Committee

Introduction Week: The CCA & First-Year Student Relationship

CCA Directions: Students should be introduced to this strategy at orientation. Students should come to the first one-on-one meeting with a draft of their learning committee communication log. The communication log is designed to help students monitor their communication efforts throughout the semester. This approach will help students develop an informed strategic communication plan for interacting with their professors. The goal is to move students from a structured communication plan to a more fluid communication plan. This exercise is also a great practice for developing or improving social networking skills, which is paramount in life after college.

Purpose: In order to develop a healthy relationship with all professors, it is imperative you **communicate effectively** with each of your professors on a regular basis. Your faculty serves as your learning committee. The learning committee will help shape your learning with direct feedback, advanced guidance, and leadership.

Sample Communication Log: *See the next page for a full example.*

	Monday	Tuesday	Wednesday	Thursday	Friday	Saturday	Sunday
Email							
Office Visit							
Conference Call							
Lunch							

*We highly recommend you communicate with your professor(s) every two weeks.

INTRODUCTION TO ACADEMIC AND SOCIAL SUCCESS

Communication Log Sheets

Week _____

	Monday	Tuesday	Wednesday	Thursday	Friday	Saturday	Sunday
Email							
Office Visit							
Conference Call							
Lunch							

Week _____

	Monday	Tuesday	Wednesday	Thursday	Friday	Saturday	Sunday
Email							
Office Visit							
Conference Call							
Lunch							

THE FIRST-YEAR COLLEGE EXPERIENCE HANDBOOK

Week _____

	Monday	Tuesday	Wednesday	Thursday	Friday	Saturday	Sunday
Email							
Office Visit							
Conference Call							
Lunch							

CHAPTER 1

The Co-Curricular Advisor & Student Relationship

"My transition from an urban inner-city environment to a very rural Methodist University could have been much more difficult without the wisdom, insight, and extremely relevant experiences in this program."

> Donald "D.J" Colvin,
> Business Unit Manager, JAC Products
> Ohio Northern University, 1994 - 1999

THE CO-CURRICULAR ADVISOR & STUDENT RELATIONSHIP

Character Development: Identifying the Best YOU!

Your Personal Talk Journal

Developing a consistent habit of reflection is an important first step in laying a foundation of academic success. It is important that you have developed a basic level of trust and expectations about the work you all will do together before you begin working with your student on the personal talk journal,. The purpose of this exercise is to assist the student in understanding how to develop a reflective habit and make connections between behavior and perception. Discuss the following questions with your student.

1. When was the last time you remember being at your best?

2. How would you describe that day, week, or moment?

3. What was going on in your life at that time?

4. What emotions do you remember and why?

5. If that time is now, how are you handling the transition?

THE FIRST-YEAR COLLEGE EXPERIENCE HANDBOOK

Academic Development: Value Inventory

Chapter 1: VALUE INVENTORY

CCA Directions: Occasionally, students overlook the value of their living-learning high school experience. Students tend not to link personal values to learning. When this occurs, personal values and learning drift apart. As a result, students resist learning and the learning environment. This reality widens the gap of engaged learning.

It is important for students to reflect on their high school experience so they gain a sense of how their personal values impact learning. This exercise will give the student an opportunity to draw from these experiences the knowledge and skills gained to strengthen study habits, organizational skills, ability to prioritize, work ethic, etc. By drawing connections between personal values and learning, students will deepen their commitment to success.

The following contain a number of values, which some students hold as more or less important. Please rate the importance of these values—how much they _impact_ your learning. Challenge yourself to rate every value. There are no right or wrong answers. When complete, discuss your rating with your CCA.

The objective of this exercise is to help students identify which values to be intentional about in their learning efforts.

They should use the list below to identify which topic is more or less important to them.

Topic	Very Valuable	Valuable	Average Value	Limited Value	Not Valuable
Curfew					
Family loss					
Sports					
Peers/Friends					
Driver's License					
Failing a test					
Dating relationship(s)					
Use or abuse of Alcohol					
Use or abuse of Drugs					
Siblings					
Traumatic events					
Self-Esteem					
High School Transcript/Grades					
Faith/Spirituality					
Eating disorders					
Personal health and wellbeing					
Social Media					
Suicide					
Gossip					
Body Image					

Debriefing questions:
1. Which selection was the most difficult to make?
2. Are there any biases or trends in your responses?
3. What have you learned about yourself?
4. How can this information be helpful throughout the semester?
5. Which response would you like to change in the near future? Why?

Academic Development: Energy Line

Chapter 1: Forming the CCA-Mentee Relationship: Energy Line
CCA DIRECTIONS:
1). Have the student draw an energy line for their busiest school day using the times at the bottom of the graph (x axis) and the energy levels on the side of the graph (y axis). Have students plot where their energy falls during different times of the day. Energy lines can take many different shapes but naturally should have highs and lows throughout the day.
2). Have the student write in their class schedule, including co-curricular activities, lunch, exercise, sleep, etc.
3). Have students *honestly* discuss how their energy impacts their productivity throughout the day. For example, if a student's energy is low at 8:00 a.m. and that is the time the student has Biology, the student is forcing his/her body to focus and concentrate when his/her body is not ready to perform. Discussion question: Should the student get up earlier? Should the student go to sleep earlier?
4). Students should use their energy line to be aware of times in which they can maximize their concentration and schedule their study time/ classes wisely. The aim of this exercise is to help students identify their peak performance time.

EXAMPLE:

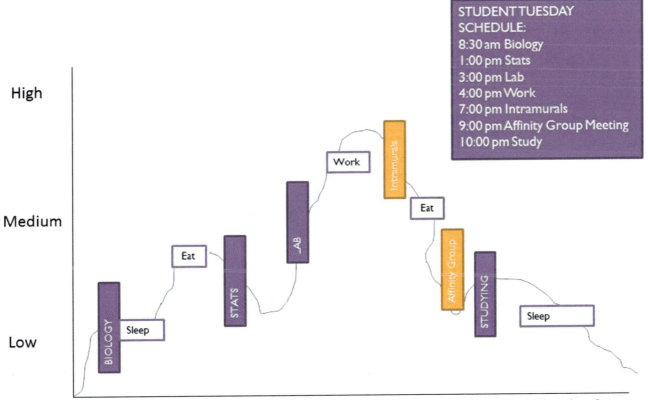

THE CO-CURRICULAR ADVISOR & STUDENT RELATIONSHIP

Academic Development: Energy Line

Chapter 1: Forming the CCA-Mentee Relationship: Energy Line

Before completing your Energy Line, consider the following:
1. *What are some of the challenges with Student A?*
2. *What changes should Student A consider?*
3. *What are some things out of the student's control?*
4. *Do you have suggestions for Student A?*

Discuss these questions with your CCA. Then give it a try for yourself.

High

Medium

Low

8am 9am 10am 11am 12pm 1pm 2pm 3pm 4pm 5pm 6pm 7pm 8pm 9pm 10pm 11pm 12am 1am 2am

Academic Development: Personal Contract

Chapter 1: Forming the CCA-Mentee Relationship
CCA Directions: In order to take more ownership over their academic and social success, students are charged to develop a self-contract. This contract should be discussed with the Co-Curricular Advisor. Students should also discuss their contracts with the Student Advocate. The Student Advocate and the Co-Curricular Advisor are students' accountability partners; they hold the student responsible for committing to clear academic standards and social behavior goals.

This document should be revisited routinely throughout the semester.

EXAMPLE:
I, _____ (name), pledge to do the following:

- ☐ Attend class regularly
- ☐ Develop a planner
- ☐ Get rest
- ☐ Eat Healthy
- ☐ Exercise
- ☐ Remove myself from unhealthy habits
- ☐ Set and achieve goals
- ☐ Complete my homework ahead of time
- ☐ Nothing to embarrass my family, friends, and community
- ☐ Respect my fellow student
- ☐ Empower others
- ☐ Be a good citizen in my community
- ☐ Communicate effectively with my Co-Curricular Advisor and Student Advocate
- ☐ Perform random acts of kindness
- ☐ Study in a timely manner

In order to avoid failure to fulfill my pledge, I will report my progress to my Co-Curricular Advisor and Student Advocate.

_____   _____   _____   _____
Student   **Student Advocate**   **Co-Curricular Advisor**   **Date**

CHAPTER 2

Getting Adjusted & Planning for Academic Success

"This program has played a vital role in the success of many students from various institutions throughout the Midwest and Southern regions of the country. This program has provided students with the academic, philosophical, and emotional tools needed to become successful and influential community members."

> Clay Sanders,
> Residence Coordinator, University of North Carolina Charlotte
>
> Assistant Director of Intercultural Programs and Residence Life,
> Buena Vista University, 2007 - 2008

> Components of this chapter was
> inspired by Stephen R. Covey

Character Development:
Around the Clock Personal Development and Self-Care

While most students are gearing up for the rigor in academia, some are more concerned with meeting the expectations of the day. In our experience, we have found that students struggle to meet personal expectations while embracing the new. If you feel overwhelmed, no don't worry: you are not alone! As you continue to become familiar with the campus, you will learn that most students are trying to find the right ingredients for meeting expectations and minimizing anxieties. *Around the Clock Personal Development and Self-Care* will challenge you to identify strategies for academic and social success.

In the diagram below, you will find our short list of personal development and self-care strategies. We selected these strategies based on our *Around the Clock* needs to perform daily tasks at the highest level of effectiveness and efficiency. Now, we want you to take a few minutes to think about your personal development and self-care needs. On a separate sheet of paper, create your *Around the Clock Personal Development and Self-Care* plan. For more assistance, follow the instructions below. Be creative and make your clock unique to you! Make sure that you share this learning experience with your Student Advocate and Co-Curricular Advisor.

* In the example below, please keep in mind that our day starts at 6:00 a.m.

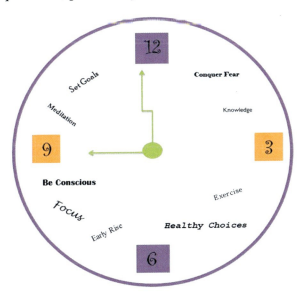

Assignment:
1. Create your Around the Clock Personal Development and Self-Care plan. Think about what you need to be successful for the day.
2. Categorize each strategy by placing *(1) academic* or *(2) social* next to the strategy. If the strategy meets both academic and social needs, place (1) and (2) where necessary.
3. Write a two-page paper describing the purpose of each strategy. Challenge yourself to elaborate on the strategies that meet both academic and social expectations.

Questions to consider:
a. What impact does my plan have on my learning?
b. What impact does my plan have on my social life?
c. What resources do I need to maintain a balanced life?
d. How will this plan help me reach my academic and social goals?

GETTING ADJUSTED & PLANNING FOR ACADEMIC SUCCESS

Academic Development: Academic Playbook: 1st and 10

Chapter 2: Academic Playbook: 1st and 10

CCA Directions: Some of the world's greatest sports fans applaud teams with great game plans and schemes. Students will not succeed without a game plan. Every game plan needs game changers. In the play sketched below, the student is the QB. Arguably the most important position on the field, the QB is responsible for knowing the opposition. The QB is also in charge of selecting the right teammate who gives the team the greatest probability of success.

Who is on your team? What positions do they play? What are their assignments? What is the greatest threat to you and your team's success? Okay, game changer! You make the call! Develop your own game plan and insert the necessary information below. On a separate sheet of paper, draw up a play and give your play a name. Be prepared to explain your play to the class/group.

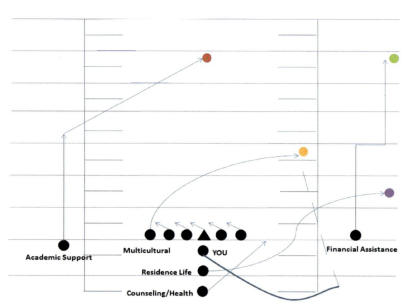

Play Call: "Yuko" - Pro Left, 28 Power, F Flat, Y-Drag

INSTRUCTION:
1. Draw up a play.
2. Identify the positions, departments, and responsibilities.
3. In the last column, name the benefits.

Department	Responsibility	Benefit
Multicultural		
Academic Support		
Residence Life		
Counseling/Health		
Financial Assistance		

DEBRIEFING:
1. Why did you select this particular teammate?
2. What does this department bring to your team?
3. Which department was left off the team? Why?

GETTING ADJUSTED & PLANNING FOR ACADEMIC SUCCESS

Academic Development: Academic Spaces

Chapter 2: Developing Relationships and Identifying Allies

CCA Directions: Grab a campus map and review the many academic buildings, residence halls, dining services, libraries, student support services, green space, lakes, or ponds. Use the campus map to broaden your perspective of the myriad of academic spaces available. It is important to note that the number of different academic spaces is not as important as the number of hours students devote to one particular space.

Many students are unaware of the number of academic spaces available to students. If you are like most students, studying in your room, lounge, library, or cafeteria allows you to study, retain, and regurgitate information in a familiar setting. The research shows that students experience great success studying in traditional academic settings. However, not all the students can go to the library at the same time. With this in mind, students have to identify new academic spaces to meet their needs.

Unlike student gathering spaces, academic spaces, such as a classroom, mirror the learning environment students are challenged to actively engage in. It is important that students study in the classroom because the classroom represents the learning context in which students will be asked to excel. In other words, students should study in an environment that is similar to their testing environment. We also recommend you select an academic space complimentary to your learning style.

In the spaces provided, name two additional academic spaces. Use the campus map to develop ideas. Consult with faculty, staff, suitemates, affinity groups, or cohorts to identify new academic spaces. Once you complete the assignment, share this information with the class.

ACADEMIC SPACES

EXAMPLE:

BY YOURSELF

1. Library
2. Classrooms
3. _____
4. _____

FEW DISTRACTIONS

1. Residence Halls Lounge
2. Lab
3. _____
4. _____

SOCIAL PLACES

1. Café
2. Affinity Space
3. _____
4. _____

GROUP

1. Outside
2. Coffee House
3. _____
4. _____

Debriefing

1. Which learning environment are you most comfortable studying in?
2. Is there a learning environment you prefer over others?
3. Is there a learning environment that complements your learning style better than others?
4. Which learning environment is less effective for you?
5. Which learning environment is detrimental to your learning style?

THINGS TO CONSIDER:

- *It is important that students are aware of hours of operation for each building.*
- *It is important that students are familiar with the amenities in each building (lounge, desk, couches, tables).*
- *It is important that students contact security for safety precautions involved in occupying each building.*

GETTING ADJUSTED & PLANNING FOR ACADEMIC SUCCESS

Academic Development: Time Pie

Chapter 2: Developing Relationships and Identifying Allies in the Classroom

CCA Directions: The purpose of this activity is to visually show students the amount of time they spend in the classroom versus outside the classroom, and how the time devoted to each area impacts their learning. Before completing this exercise, students should think about the time they spend in classes, studying, working, exercising, and socializing. Make sure students include personal and fun time.

We have found that students have different time commitments due to their interests. Regardless of where your academic and social endeavors lead you, managing your time is key to success. This exercise is designed to help students calculate their daily activities.

Instructions: The time pie represents 24 hours. The shape of your pie slice(s) should be representative of the amount of time committed to studying, class, exercise, etc. To deepen the conversation, ask students to apply a percentage to each activity/insertion. Some slices of your pie will be smaller or larger than others. Do not exceed 24 hours.

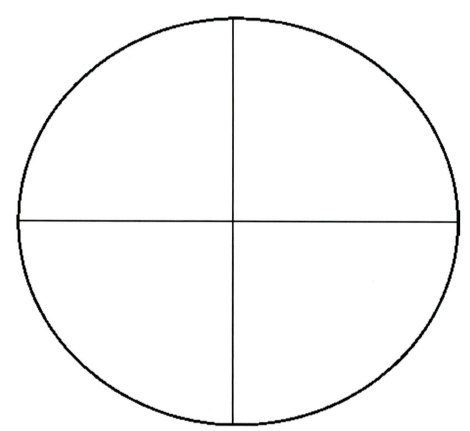

Consider the following experiences as you draw your time pie:

Studying	Meal Times	Weekly Meetings
Hobbies	Attending Class	Sleeping
Exercise	Socializing	Watching TV
Social Media	Job	Personal Time (shower, laundry, etc.)
Relationship	Community Service	Affinity Group

Debriefing Questions:

1. What is your overall observation of your time pie?
2. Does your time pie reflect the outcomes you are seeking?
3. Are there any areas needing immediate attention?

Now What?
1. What are your immediate, intermediate, and long-term goals?
2. What resources are needed to help you achieve your goals?

GETTING ADJUSTED & PLANNING FOR ACADEMIC SUCCESS

Academic Development: Time-Wasters

Chapter 2: Developing Relationships and Identifying Allies in the Classroom

CCA Directions: Many first-year students enter college with some knowledge as to how to balance their classes, homework, finances, job, friends, and relationships. On the other hand, some students do not know how to manage their time well. Managing time well is very important to the academic and social success of students. More importantly, managing time-wasters is keys to sustaining academic and social success.

Identifying time-wasters will allow you to understand the difference between productive and nonproductive ways to manage your time outside the classroom. We believe there is strength in both, but there is greater strength and reward in identifying nonproductive time management. In our experience, students who have successfully identified nonproductive time management commitments have minimized distractions that hinder their academic and social growth.

In the exercise below, you are asked to identify the activities or commitments that compete for your attention. This activity should bring to light time wasters that threaten your overall academic success and character development.

Special Note: After completing the exercise, please answer the questions to help you process your learning.

TIME WASTERS

Check all that apply as your biggest time wasters:

_____ Surfing the internet
_____ Social Media
_____ Talking on the phone
_____ Procrastination
_____ Not prioritizing tasks
_____ Inability to say "No" to an opportunity
_____ Not using a list of things to do
_____ Unorganized desk, work space, or study space
_____ Email
_____ Television
_____ Video games
_____ Socializing with friends
_____ Studying with too many distractions (radio, TV, IM, door open, etc.)
_____ Mental breaks from studying that turn into mental vacations
_____ Inability to decipher class notes
_____ Finding other things to do in your room (laundry, alphabetize CDs, IM, etc.)
_____ Sleeping during the day
_____ Random trips to Wal-Mart, Target, bookstore, etc. that take too long
_____ Trying to accomplish too much at once
_____ Other:

Debriefing Questions:
1. What do you observe about your answers?
2. How concerned are you about your responses?
3. What must you do to balance your academic and social life?
4. What are you most proud of?
5. What are you least proud of?
6. What will be your mindset moving forward?
7. What would you like to change?

THE FIRST-YEAR COLLEGE EXPERIENCE HANDBOOK

Academic Development: Time Management

Chapter 2: Developing Relationships and Identifying Allies in the Classroom

CCA Directions: The purpose of this activity is to help students visually organize their time and see where they can be more productive daily. It is important that students are able to see the big picture of their workloads in and out of the classroom. Instruct students to leave nothing out as they complete this exercise. Make sure they include topics such as exercise, tests, projects, presentations, papers, affinity meeting times, and personal time.

Be creative: use color coding or other methods to emphasize importance and relevance. For example, you may indicate that you call home every day at 6:00 p.m. If calling home is of great importance to you, you may place an asterisk beside that block of time indicating that this commitment is a MUST. As you complete this exercise, take into consideration that this is not futuristic. This is your reality NOW! No one knows what you need, when you need it, and how often you need it in order to accomplish your academic goals and further develop your character.

Complete the chart below indicating your commitments throughout the day. Discuss with your CCA your thought process and approach to generating positive results in the classroom. Also, discuss the strength and weakness of your schedule. We recommend you revisit this schedule after mid-terms to record changes in your schedule.

Lastly, many students enjoy the color coding process because it is a very reflective exercise and a lot of fun. However, many students struggle to follow their schedule. For instance, you schedule lunch for 90 minutes but you sit and talk to friends after eating for 2 hours, which compromises your study time and impacts your meeting time. Ultimately, this leads to cramming and procrastination, which more often leads to below average performance in the classroom. It is purposeless to make a schedule and not follow it.

GETTING ADJUSTED & PLANNING FOR ACADEMIC SUCCESS

Tips for Color Coding

1. Select a color to designate class times. Block out class times on the schedule.
2. Select another color for eating times. Block out eating on the schedule.
3. Select another color for standing meetings (ex: Advising, BSC, intramural sports, working out). Block out that time on the schedule.
4. Select another color for study time. Block out study time.

Time Management

	Sunday	Monday	Tuesday	Wednesday	Thursday	Friday	Saturday
8:00am							
9:00am							
10:00am							
11:00am							
Noon							
1:00pm							
2:00pm							
3:00pm							
4:00pm							
5:00pm							
6:00pm							
7:00pm							
8:00pm							
9:00pm							
10:00pm							
11:00pm							

Academic Development: Time Management Matrix

Chapter 2: Developing Relationships and Identifying Allies in the Classroom

CCA Directions: The purpose of this activity is to categorize time management efforts. Drawing from the previous two exercises, have students insert below those items that are: 1) Important/urgent; 2) Important/not urgent; 3) Not important/urgent; and 4) Not important/not urgent. This is a fun, thought-provoking exercise that will help students notice things that complement academic and social development and eliminate or minimize commitments that inhibit their ability to reach their goals.

Using the previous exercises, help students prioritize the concept of Time. The four quadrants will be used by the student to determine the tasks with the highest importance, decide which tasks need to be a priority, and determine which tasks need to be eliminated.

Special Note: Ask students to insert information from their time pie and time waster sheet inside the boxes below.

Important/Urgent	Important/Not Urgent
Not Important/Urgent	Not Important/Not Urgent

GETTING ADJUSTED & PLANNING FOR ACADEMIC SUCCESS

In an effort to avoid not placing value on the items that hold dear to your heart, we have decided to refrain from providing examples. However, we have provided a short description of each quadrant to help you categorize things appropriately.

Quadrant 1: Important, urgent
(Requiring immediate attention)

Quadrant 2: Important but not urgent
(Not requiring immediate attention)

Quadrant 3: Urgent but Unimportant
(Items to be minimized)

Quadrant 4: unimportant and not urgent
(Items to be eliminated)

PRIORITY	MINIMIZED	ELIMINATED

This diagram has been adopted from Stephen R. Covey's "The Seven Habits of Highly Effective People" for the benefit of this document.

CHAPTER 3

Academic and Social Peaks and Valleys

Just like many of you, coming into college I was excited about getting started with the next step of my life. I was also nervous about whether or not I'd figure out what I was destined to do and if I'd be successful in my academic studies. This academic program at Buena Vista University allowed me to not only recognize my academic potential and prowess, but it also helped me build character. With continual encouragement, support, and guidance, this program opened my mind to the world of opportunity: the world in which I could use my education to lay the foundation for my future success. I graduated in 2009 from Buena Vista University, Summa Cum Laude, and I attribute a large part of my success to this program!

      Phylicia Proctor,
      Federal Collaboration and Smarter Workforce Solutions Software Consultant,
      IBM
      Buena Vista University, 2004-2009

ACADEMIC AND SOCIAL PEAKS AND VALLEYS

Character Development: The Blueprint for Managing Goals

In your first year of college, you will engage in co-curricular activities that may compete with the classroom for your attention. It is important to note here that we are not suggesting co-curricular activities are distractions. Instead, we are suggesting *unmanaged* co-curricular activities are distractions. First-year students with goals, action strategies, and processes have experienced more success in managing the outcomes.

In the diagram below, you will find a blueprint to help you turn your vision into reality. It is important that you know precisely what you want to achieve so you can concentrate your efforts more strategically. This approach will also help you identify any distractions that deter you from success.

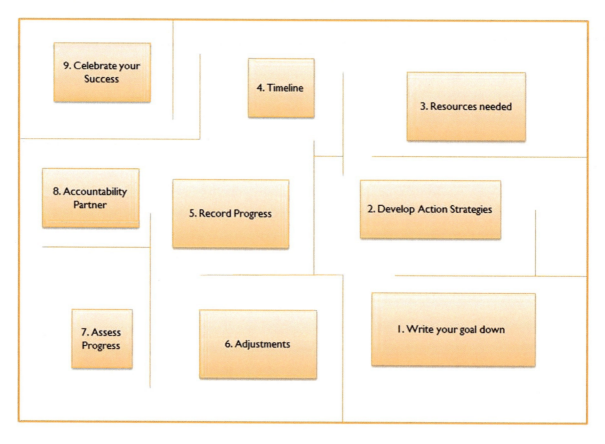

1. **Goal Setting:** It is very important that you write down your goal(s). Each goal deserves its own blueprint. Remember to be specific and realistic. The goal will serve as the guide for all other things you do to reach it.

2. **Action strategies:** Take a minute to imagine what's next. Ask yourself: Who? What? Where? Why? How? Now what? These will determine the steps that will lead you to the goal.

3. **Resources:** What resources are needed to help you move closer to your goal(s)? Which department on campus can help you advance in reaching your goal? Who has already accomplished what you want to accomplish, and what steps did they take?

4. **Timeline:** Every goal needs a timeline. A timeline is a great way to build progress reports. Develop a timeline that includes short, intermediate, and long-term action strategies.

5. **Record Progress:** Having an honest conversation about your growth in college is one of the most difficult things to do in your first year. There are many ways to evaluate growth. We recommend journaling, writing a self-reflection letter, or creating a memoir (e.g., How am I doing? Have I maximized my resources? Am I sticking to my timeline?).

6. **Adjustments:** After taking a preliminary look at your progress, make any necessary adjustments to ensure you are on track to reach your goal.

7. **Assess Progress:** After making minor adjustments, ask yourself: Am I on the right path to achieve my goal? What can I do differently? Take time to seek out advice from someone you respect who can give you feedback on your progress.

8. **Accountability Partner:** Identify someone in your circle who can hold you accountable! This should be someone who will be honest with you no matter what and will give you the feedback you need to help you grow.

9. **Celebrate:** Students fail too often to celebrate personal success. Treat yourself to your favorite food, take a small trip, or visit a loved one.

ACADEMIC AND SOCIAL PEAKS AND VALLEYS

Goal
Action Strategies: 1. 2. 3.
Resources: NAME　　　　　　　　　　DEPARTMENT　　　　　　　　　SERVICE 1. 2. 3. 4.
Timeline ⟵――――――――――――――――⟶
Adjustments: 1. 2. 3.

Academic Development: Academic Goals

Chapter 3: Developing and Maintaining Relationships

CCA Advisor Directions: Students often store their academic goals in their minds, and, for many reasons, we are ill-equipped to discuss these goals with them. Although the reasons are numerous, we have found one of the major reasons why students don't reach their goals is that students fail to write them down.

Now that you have a sense of the academic culture on your campus, it is time to write down your academic goals. Writing down your goals is a powerful exercise that will enrich your academic experience. By writing down your goals, you will discover that goal-setting also builds character.

Grade Point Average: It is important that you establish a grade point average and earn the grade you expect in each class. Have an HONEST conversation with your CCA about expected performance in each class. In week 5, have a realistic conversation with your CCA about your current grade *(Is there a difference between the expected grade in Week 3 and Week 5)*. At midterms discuss the progress or lack thereof in each course. Specifically, discuss results and write concerns in the space provided.

CCAs: Throughout the remainder of the semester, please ask students about their personal goals, academic goals, career goals, and life aspirations. This document will be revisited after mid-terms and before final exams.

Special Note: This is a working document. You will revisit this document in Chapter 5 and Chapter 9.

Five Reasons Why?

1. *Because your attitude and approach to learning matters!*

2. *Because written goals are personal contracts.*

3. *Because you will be motivated throughout the semester to take action.*

4. *Because you can minimize distractions.*

5. *Because we all need reminders of our purpose.*

ACADEMIC AND SOCIAL PEAKS AND VALLEYS

NAME:	MAJOR:		MINOR:		
	CLASS 1	CLASS 2	CLASS 3	CLASS 4	CLASS 5
At the end of the semester, what will your final grade be? (letter grade or percentage)					
After mid-terms, what will be your grade in each class? (letter grade or percentage)					
Currently, what is your grade in each class?					
Are you on course to reach your academic goals?					

1. What concerns do you have leading into mid-terms?
2. How can you attain your academic goals?
3. If you had to start over, what would you change (study habits, eating, sleeping, etc…)?
4. What challenges are beyond your control?
5. What resources are available to you in support of your academic goals?
6. What are your expectations for the end of the semester?

Academic Development: Personal Asset Mapping

Chapter 3: Developing and Maintaining Relationships

CCA Directions: The purpose of Personal Asset Mapping is to understand how personal assets are connected to academic goals. We define personal assets as the total value of a person's circle of influence. In other words, personal assets are things or people who have impacted an individual's growth and development. The personal asset map also serves as a visual guide to how a person's assets are interrelated.

As you design your personal asset map, feel free to change your intersecting circles. Not all personal asset maps are the same. To help you determine your circles, consider four areas that have helped you concentrate on achieving your academic goals. It is highly recommended that these persons or things have a proven record of success on your life. This is not a hypothetical exercise.

The diagram below will help you visualize the value of your personal assets while discovering what you draw from their influence on your life. The goal here is to make sure that in the midst of your college experience you do not ignore the people or things that have shaped your life.

ACADEMIC AND SOCIAL PEAKS AND VALLEYS

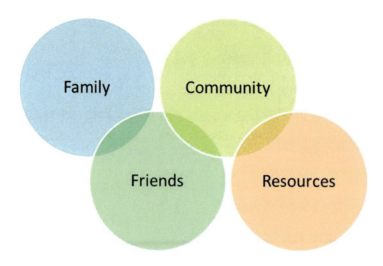

On a separate sheet of paper, draw your personal asset map. Then, write each topic in the boxes below. Next, in detail, explain why each topic is an asset to your growth and development. Lastly, describe what you need in order to sustain the relationship. In the summary, explain how these resources or relationships will impact your overall pursuit of academic excellence.

Topic	Asset	Resource/Relationships (WHAT DO YOU NEED?)
Example: *Family*	*Strong support over the years, we are very close*	*I need to go home at least once or twice a month*
Summary:		

Part 2 Academic Readiness

The Frog

When a tadpole hatches out of its egg, it feeds on tiny plants. As it grows, it begins to eat small water animals and dead fish. Its back legs grow first, followed by its front legs. The tail does not fall off but is absorbed by the body.

Students are like frogs: they spend a great deal of time learning about self. They grow into the gifts they have in preparation for adulthood. We believe that everything you need is already part of you. You just have to take advantage of every opportunity, big or small.

CHAPTER 4

Unveil Your Brain Power & Discover the Learner in You

"This program allowed me to be able to see the importance of my education at Elon and the impact that it would not only have on myself but on those who have influenced me in the past, present and future. This program was one of the many reasons that I was able to graduate from Elon University, and it helped provide an experience that will stay with me for the rest of my life. I am grateful to have had the opportunity presented to me to be a student in the Academic Enrichment Program and am grateful for the way it shaped my academic career at Elon."

> Deanna Fox,
> Assistant Director, Multicultural Center, Elon University
> Elon University, 2009 – 2013

> Components of this chapter was
> inspired by John H. Flavell

Character Development: Thinking About Thinking

If your college experience is anything like ours, you are finding new ways to think, new ways to relate, and new ways to question. However, first-year students have a tendency to overlook the power of "Now!" in their first semester. Students who understand new ways to process learning have become masters of the "Now!"

Below you will find discussion topics to help you start thinking in the "Now!" These prompts are guides to a deeper understanding of the college experience. Utilize these gestures to ignite a profitable conversation with your Student Advocate.

Discussion Topics:

1. **Be Present in the Moment.** Throughout the day, try to concentrate on the moment: who is present, who is speaking, where are you, who is moving, conversation temperament, traffic, etc.

2. **Be a Witness to Your Learning.** Pay close attention to the information you are learning and regurgitating. Ask yourself how much information you are retaining. Reward yourself for small victories.

3. **Know When To Say "When!"** Your body sends you signals that danger is approaching. Listen to your body and make adjustments in your lifestyle. You may find your peers assume they have to do everything and be everywhere in order to be successful. Although this may be your campus culture, it is in your best interest to set limitations and boundaries!

4. **Monitor What You Are Doing and When.** Active thinking is a great exercise while engaging in conversation or physical activity.

5. **Maximize Your Day.** Concentrate on making the most of your daily activities. Protect yourself from unhealthy and unproductive conversations or activities.

6. **Take a Timeout.** Take a break from the day to breathe and think clearly. Try to remove all movement, noise, and distraction around you. This habit will help you keep everything in balance.

7. **Reconnect.** Recharge your mind by identifying healthy conversations and activities to reconnect.

Academic Development: Metacognition

Metacognition refers to a learner's automatic awareness of knowledge and ability to understand, control, and manipulate his/her own cognitive processes. Metacognitive skills are important in school and throughout life. For example, Mumford (1986) says it is essential that an effective manager be a person who has learned to learn. He describes this person as one who knows the stages in the process of learning and understands his or her own preferred approaches to it—a person who can identify and overcome blocks to learning and can bring learning from outside the job into on-the-job situations.

As you read this section, do not worry about distinguishing between metacognitive skills and some of the other terms in this chapter. Metacognition overlaps heavily with some of these other terms. The terminology simply supplies another useful way to look at thought processes.

Metacognition is a relatively new field, and theorists have not yet settled on conventional terminology. However, according to Flavell (1987), most metacognitive research falls within the following categories:

1. *Metamemory.* This refers to learners' awareness of and knowledge about their own memory systems and strategies for using their memories effectively. Metamemory includes (a) awareness of different memory strategies, (b) knowledge of which strategy to use for a particular memory task, and (c) knowledge of how to use each memory strategy most effectively.

2. *Metacomprehension.* This term refers to learners' ability to monitor the degree to which they understand information being communicated to them, recognize failures to comprehend, and effectively employ repair strategies when failures are identified.

    Learners with poor metacomprehension skills often finish reading passages without even knowing they did not understand them at all. On the other hand, learners who are more adept at metacomprehension will check for confusion or inconsistency and undertake a corrective strategy, such as rereading, relating one part of the passage to another, looking for topic sentences or summary paragraphs, or relating the current information to prior knowledge (See Harris et al., 1988).

3. *Self-Regulation.* This term refers to learners' ability to make adjustments in their own learning processes in response to feedback. The concept of self-regulation overlaps heavily with the preceding two terms; its focus is on the ability of the learners themselves to monitor their own learning (without external stimuli or persuasion) and to maintain the attitudes necessary to invoke and employ these strategies on their own. To learn most effectively, students should understand what strategies are available and the purposes these strategies will serve and also become capable of adequately selecting, employing, monitoring, and evaluating their use of these strategies. (See Hallahan et al., 1979; Graham & Harris, 1992; Reid & Harris, 1989, 1993.)

Chapter 4: Meta-cognition

CCA Directions: Metacognition is *thinking and knowing* about *thinking and knowing*. It sounds bizarre, but true metacognition is studying and processing information at the same time. Take reading for instance. Metacognition allows the reader to comprehend and regulate what is being read. Metacognition can also be used to help students with memory. For example, students are required to memorize a great deal of information throughout the semester. We consider that phase of learning the thinking phase. The information cycles through the brain seeking refuge. Once the information is stored away, its shelf life shifts from thinking to knowing, which is important to memory recall.

Thinking and knowing are important abilities for processing learning. Thinking and knowing are also important abilities for life after college. Most employers are searching for undergraduates who can think and know with very little instruction and direction. Metacognition will help you better understand yourself and those around you, which makes for a great learning or working environment.

In the space provided, please indicate which statement applies to you. Discuss your selection with your CCA. The knowledge gained in this exercise is transferrable, meaning you will be able to utilize this new knowledge of self in other study areas of development.

Meta-Cognition Checklist

READING
- ____ I develop a plan before reading.
- ____ I monitor my understanding of text (make connections, use context clues).
- ____ I evaluate my thoughts after reading.
- ____ I recognize predictions in the text.
- ____ I am able to store away pertinent information.
- ____ I can recall information if necessary.

PLANNING
- ____ I think about the subject of the class.
- ____ I ask myself about causes and effects.
- ____ I concentrate on the sequence of events.
- ____ I search for problems and solutions.
- ____ I know an action is required of me.

UNVEIL YOUR BRAIN POWER & DISCOVER THE LEARNER IN YOU

LEARNING

___ I recognize when my mind begins to wander, and I am no longer reminding myself to pay attention
___ Sometime I can't remember what I just read
___ I can't answer the questions at the end of the reading
___ I can't formulate my own questions
___ I can't remember what was previously read

EVALUATING (What method do you use?)

___ I am most effective in studying when I highlight important information.
___ I am a more effective student when I take notes.
___ I can remember massive amounts of information when I read aloud.
___ I can recall information more easily when it is stored in categories.

DEBRIEFING QUESTIONS:

1. What have you learned about your approach to reading?

2. How can you improve your planning?

3. What new information have you gained about your learning style?

4. How can the new information you learned benefit your life outside the classroom?

5. Which evaluation method has proven most effective for you?

CHAPTER 5

Strategies for Success & Valuing the Learning Experience

"This program enabled us to create systems of support for students in a new way. It provided a direct line to professional staff, while developing academic relationships with students in your clubs and organizations who may not have been in your major."

>Dr. Ashley Farmer-Hanson,
>Director of Civic Engagement, Buena Vista University
>Buena Vista University, 2003 - 2007

STRATEGIES FOR SUCCESS & VALUING THE LEARNING EXPERIENCE

Character Development: Choosing to Learn to Succeed

One of the most difficult things to do is continue process learning when you are experiencing success. Most people assess learning after they experience success, such as a good score on a quiz or test, but we rarely examine learning *while* we are learning. Conversations about learning in success will deepen the success you're experiencing. Moreover, this approach will allow you to make new meaning of learning and success.

Your Personal Journal

Here are several questions to consider as you reflect on your learning. Choose two or more questions to write about.

1. How do you define learning?

2. How do you define success?

3. How do you know you are learning?

4. How do you know you are experiencing success?

5. In what ways does your learning influence your success?

Academic Development: Personal Value Assessment

Chapter 5: Unveil Your Brain Power and Discover the Learner in YOU!
CCA Advisor Directions: The Personal Value Assessment is an exercise designed to help students examine how attitude and approach to the classroom impact the learning process. Students' values are informed decisions to accept or reject a belief system. Personal values are inherited values designed to advance one's life or the life of others. Personal values allow students to sharpen their perspective of self, while drawing connections with others.

From the list below, choose ten (10) values and write them in the space provided. You may add other values that are not listed. After writing your top ten (10) choices, check (√) five (5) that are most important to you. Then, indicate in the third column which of these five (5) values you share with others.

1. ___ACHIEVEMENT (sense of accomplishment by means of skill, practice, or perseverance)
2. ___ADVANCEMENT (moving forward in your career through promotions)
3. ___ADVENTURE (work which frequently involves risk taking)
4. ___AESTHETICS (studying or appreciating the beauty of ideas, things, etc…)
5. ___AUTONOMY (working independently, determining the nature of your work without significant direction from others)
6. ___CARING (love, affection)
7. ___CHALLENGE (stimulating full use of your potential)
8. ___CHANGE & VARIETY (diverse, frequently changing work responsibilities and/or work settings)
9. ___COMPETITION (pitting your abilities against others where there is a clear win/lose outcome)
10. ___COOPERATION (opportunity to work as a team toward common goals)
11. ___CREATIVITY (being imaginative, innovative)
12. ___ECONOMIC SECURITY (having enough money)
13. ___EXCITEMENT (experiencing a high degree of or frequent excitement in your work)
14. ___FAMILY HAPPINESS (being able to spend quality time and develop relationships with family)
15. ___FRIENDHSIP (developing close personal relationships)
16. ___HEALTH (physical and psychological wellbeing)
17. ___HELP OTHERS (being involved in helping people in a direct way, individually or in group.)
18. ___HELP SOCIETY (doing something to contribute to the betterment of the world)
19. ___INNER HARMONY (being at peace with oneself)
20. ___INTERGRITY (sincerity and honesty)
21. ___INTELLECTUAL STATUS (being regarded as an expert in your field)
22. ___KNOWLEDGE (understanding gained through study and experience)
23. ___LEADERSHIP (having influence over others)
24. ___LEISURE (having time for hobbies, sports, activities and interests)
25. ___LOCATION (working in a place conducive to your lifestyle that allows you to do the things you enjoy most)
26. ___LOYALTY (steadfastness and allegiance)
27. ___PLEASURE (enjoyment)
28. ___POWER (authority)
29. ___PRECISION (working in situations where there is little tolerance for error)
30. ___RESPONSIBILITY (being accountable for results)
31. ___RECOGNITION (getting acknowledged for your contribution)
32. ___STABIILITY (having a predictable work routine and duties that are not likely to change over a long period of time)

STRATEGIES FOR SUCCESS & VALUING THE LEARNING EXPERIENCE

33. ___SPIRTUALITY (participating in spiritual rituals, customs and traditions)
34. ___TIME FREEDOM (working according to your own time schedule with no specific work hours required)
35. ___WEALTH (profiting, making a lot of money)
36. ___WISDOM (understanding based on accumulation of knowledge)

Value	Most Important	Share with others

Debriefing:

1. Did you already have a clear grasp of your values, or did you discover something in the process of this exercise?

2. How did you arrive at your choices?

3. Why are these values important to you?

4. What are the benefits of sharing your values with others?

5. How can commonality and difference between your values and the values of others be beneficial to your academic growth and development?

Academic Development: Reading the Environment

Chapter 5: Social and Emotional Learning: Evaluating the Growth Process

CCA Advisor Directions: Regardless of students' level of comfort or confidence in the classroom, many first-year students perform below their potential because they underestimate the academic rigor in college. Besides the lengthy homework assignments, group projects, and expanded study hours, performing proficiently among peers is one of the greatest roadblocks to the academic success of first-year students.

It is important for students to assess their learning environment adequately in order to effectively persist without experiencing inferiority. In our experience, inferiority is a threat that widens the gap between you and your academic goals. One of the ways to address inferiority is to have an honest conversation about students' perception of the learning environment.

Below you will find a short survey designed to help you examine how you interact with your learning environment in order to perform at the highest level of success. There are no right or wrong answers. Upon completion of the survey, please take a moment to answer the debriefing questions.

	Strongly Agree	Agree	Disagree	Strongly Disagree
I feel my high school learning experience prepared me for college				
I feel capable of success in the classroom				
I feel confident in the classroom				
My success in college is linked to the success of my peers				
I feel intimidated in the classroom				
I feel uncomfortable contacting my professor				
I feel like the professor speaks down to me				

Special Note: Please remember to revisit your Academic Goals sheet.

STRATEGIES FOR SUCCESS & VALUING THE LEARNING EXPERIENCE

Debriefing Questions: *On a separate sheet of paper, please answer the following questions.*

1. What new perspective(s) have you gained about your approach to learning?

2. How are you adjusting to your learning environment?

3. How do you plan to use the campus resources to be successful in the classroom?

4. Who are you comfortable speaking with in regards to your concerns?

5. What community resources are available to you?

Academic Development: Mind Mapping

Chapter 5: Evaluating the Growth Process

CCA Directions: Most mind maps are used to link and arrange preparation of studying. While this is a very useful tactic to studying, we have found that mind mapping is also a great tool for tracking social and personal involvement. When it comes to studying, the elements of studying are arranged intuitively according to importance. In this exercise, students will examine the challenges of developing strong study skills, while evaluating what is competing for their time. This is not bad competition. This is just the reality of the world and we recognize that all things, outside of studying matter.

In our experience, we have found that students memorize information via shapes and images, but too often these shapes and images are flooded with other information. As a result, preparation for academic success competes with other information. Instead of attempting to work within competing agendas, prioritize and categorize each topic. The prompts below will help you imagine what is competing for your time. Remember, we are examining the totality of your experience.

Mind Mapping

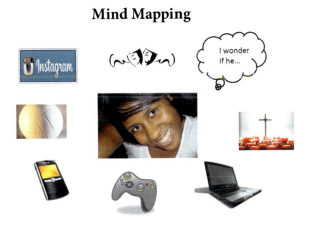

* On a separate sheet of paper, create your own mind map to help you understand what is competing for your time. Be creative!

Academic:
1. Which item(s) poses the greatest threat to your academic success?
2. In what ways is this item threatening to your academic success?
3. Create a mind map for academics. What is competing for your time?

Social:
1. Which item(s) consumes most of your free time?
2. In what ways is this item helpful or harmful? Why?
3. Create a mind map of your social life. Keep in mind that there are a number of healthy ways to be involved on campus. What is pulling you away from these healthy opportunities?

Relationships:
1. How do you connect with family, friends, and important people in your life?
2. On a daily or weekly basis, how much time is devoted to the relationship?
3. Create a mind map that features the important people in your life, the nature of the relationship, and the means of your communication with them.

STRATEGIES FOR SUCCESS & VALUING THE LEARNING EXPERIENCE

ASSESSMENT
What are the strengths of your mind maps?
What are you learning about yourself?
What is competing for your time?
What threats are hindering your progress?
What methods and strategies can you use to redirect your attention?
What is the most direct path you can take to accomplish your academic goals?
What strategies have you used in the past to accomplish your goals?
Do you feel overwhelmed or fragmented?
Now what?

Strategic Plan:

Vision. What is your vision for yourself? Who do you want to be?

Mission. Create a mission statement. What is your purpose?

Values. What do you believe? (Revisit your personal value assessment, if necessary)

Strategy. What is your goal and how will you get there?

CHAPTER 6

Mid-term Prep & Meaningful Experiences and Relationships

"The Academic Enrichment Program served as a road map for my academic success. As a student in the program my freshman year, I appreciated the faculty and staff involvement paired with a student mentor component. As coordinator for AEP my senior year, I saw the academic progress in myself as well as the engagement and impression it leaves on the student."

> Shakinah Simeona,
> Admissions Counselor at Pfeiffer University
> Elon University, 2008 - 2012

MID-TERM PREP & MEANINGFUL EXPERIENCES AND RELATIONSHIPS

Character Development: Academic Road Trip

This is a fun exercise to discuss with your Student Advocate or your classmates. In pairs or a group, brainstorm ideas about your Academic Road Trip. Once you brainstorm ideas, map out a road trip to graduation. If you want to achieve a short-term goal, you may consider the end of your first-year as a destination. It's your call! Be sure to summarize your experience thoroughly. On poster board, use images, buttons, pictures, M&M's, toothpicks, magazine clippings, or other items to create your Academic Road trip. The prompts below will help you chart your course of success. Be creative and have fun. Be prepared to provide an explanation for your road trip.

1. Determine the Destination.
Decide if your academic road trip is for next semester, next year, or graduation.
What knowledge and skills have you gained that you are willing to take with you on your trip?

2. Decide which Route.
After you name your destination, decide which route gives you the best opportunity to arrive at your destination. What classes, electives, departments, co-curricular experiences, and affinity groups will ensure a less-stressful journey?

3. Perform Maintenance.
Before every trip, it is important to fully service your vehicle prior to departure. Similarly, you have to check all of your vitals to make certain you are prepared for the journey.

4. Check Weather Conditions.
It is important for you to check your learning environment for rain, snow, or tornadoes. Students often struggle when they are confronted with unplanned, untimely circumstances. Is your academic setting conducive to learning?

5. Supplies.
Do you have the necessary supplies/resources to increase the success of your journey?

6. Rest Areas.
Along the way, plan to stop at rest areas. It is important to take a break or simply catch your breath. Your journey will involve different speed zones: 35, 55, 65, or 70. Every change in speed warrants rest.

7. Cooler of Goodies.
Along the way, reward yourself for the hard work you have committed to the journey. A reward system will revitalize you when you feel like you are not moving at the speed you desire.

8. Emergency Stops.
Unfortunately, there will times when you experience setbacks and delays. Are you prepared for the traffic jams of life that may disrupt your pursuit of excellence?

9. Give a Copy of Your Plans to a Trusted Friend.

For accountability purposes and in case of emergencies, share your plan with a friend, mentor, or advisor.

10. Reserve Driver.

Identify a peer (mentor, tutor, etc…) who can alleviate stress before you become exhausted, burned-out, or overwhelmed.

Academic Development: Mid-term Preparation

Chapter 6: Things Students Need to Know
CCA Directions: Preparing for a test can be one of the most frightening things for any student. With this in mind, we do not intend to amplify anxieties. In fact, we plan to validate what students are experiencing and then provide students with some helpful hints to reduce anxiety.

Keep in mind, this is your first college mid-term, and what you are experiencing is real. Do not ignore what you are feeling, be it excitement or fear. It is important to pause here because emotions that are unguarded tend to migrate to other areas of your development if ignored. Tests or major projects are not the root cause of anxiety. In fact, tests or major projects exploit unresolved issues in your life.

With this in mind, examine the totality of your living-learning experience to help you plan for success. In the diagram below, you will find six (6) approaches to mid-term preparation. Each preparation tactic has been designed to help you to reduce your anxieties and enhance your academic readiness. Examine these principles and decide which one(s) will better prepare you for success.

SIX PRINCIPLES OF MID-TERM PREPARATION

Emotional Preparation	Spiritual Preparation	Physical Preparation
Social Preparation	Occupational Preparation	Intellectual Preparation

Social Preparation
1. Minimize your role in your organizations to accomplish your goals.
2. Manage your weekend commitments more effectively.
3. Balance your time to include rest.

Physical Preparation
1. Exercise with regularity (e.g., walk, run, weight-lift).
2. Manage your eating habits (e.g., water, antioxidants, dry fruit, nuts).
3. Visit the health center for a check-up.
4. Take time for relaxation or meditation.
5. What is your body saying to you?

Emotional Preparation
1. Keep a positive attitude and approach.
2. Do not neglect your feelings.
3. Meditate for stress-reduction.
4. Know when to ask for help.

Intellectual Preparation
1. Know your strengths and under-developments.
2. Focus on listening and note-taking.
3. Stay ahead of your syllabus.
4. Diversify your intellectual wisdom.

Spiritual Preparation
1. Spend time deepening your personal values.
2. Increase your spiritual rituals, customs, and traditions.
3. Participate in spiritual cleansing services.
4. Contact spiritual leaders for consultation.

Occupational
1. Limit work hours.
2. Refrain from taking-on additional hours.
3. Review notes during downtime.

DEVELOP A MID-TERM PLAN: *What areas of preparation do you need to monitor closely. Why?*

☐ _____
☐ _____
☐ _____
☐ _____
☐ _____
☐ _____
☐ _____

MID-TERM PREP & MEANINGFUL EXPERIENCES AND RELATIONSHIPS

On a broader scale, write a goal for each area of development and how it impacts your academic goals and character. Discuss your answers with your Co-Curricular Advisor.

WELL-BEING	GOAL	How does this goal help you achieve your academic goal?	How does this goal help build your character?
SOCIAL			
INTELLECTUAL			
PHYSICAL			
SPIRITUAL			
OCCUPATIONAL			
EMOTIONAL			

Academic Development: Transferrable Skills

Chapter 6: Things Students Need to Know

CCA Directions: Much like the job market, recognizing transferrable skills is a value added to the learning experience. It is important to know what skills are most likely to impact academic success. Equally important is knowing what skills need further development. By this point in the semester, students have a working knowledge of what it takes to fully engage in homework assignments and group projects. Students are familiar with the challenges of balancing work, study, class, and life. Students have a greater understanding of good study habits. Now they have to decide which skills are beneficial to carry into the next semester and which skills are secondary or are in need of more development.

It is important to note that transferable skills can be academic and social skills. When we speak of transferrable skills, we are referring to the academic YOU and social YOU! In the diagram below, you will find two columns marked "developed and underdeveloped" skills. Follow the prompts closely and write down your answers in the space provided.

Developed Skills	Underdeveloped Skills
Example: Critical Thinking Writing Business Etiquette	Example: Public Speaking Integrity Research Methods
Developed (What you do well?)	**Underdeveloped (What needs improvement?)**
Strengthen (How can you strengthen your developed skills?)	**Strengthen (How can you improve your underdevelopments?)**
Resources (What resources do you need for improvements?)	**Resources (What resources do you need for improvements?)**

Part 3: Academic and Social Reflection

The Bee

Bees visit flowers for a drink of nectar and pick up pollen from the stamens as they climb inside the flower. The pollen is carried to another flower by the insect.

Great students are like bees: they feed and grow in one setting and carry that learning to a new setting. Some of the skills include, study habits, prioritization, time management, setting and meeting deadlines, among others. In the end, students draw from these experiences to deepen their purpose in any new learning environment.

CHAPTER 7

Crucial Conversations in Diverse Settings

"It can easily be admitted that this program, formerly Academic Enrichment Program (AEP), has been instrumental to my academic and personal development at Elon University. As a freshman, I was paired with Co-Curricular Advisor, Professor Nancy Midgette. With her help, I was able to adjust my academic aspirations with the academic realities of college life. Her guidance, with the assistance of the AEP manual, helped me develop the skills to maintain an accurate calendar, become involved in the *Life Entrepreneurship* program, and pursue my intellectual interest at Elon without intimidation. To this day, I continue to use the lessons I learned while in the AEP program."

Immanuel Bryant, Men of Character
Graduate of Elon University, Class of 2014
Major: Education

Components of this chapter was
inspired by Robert J. Nash

THE FIRST-YEAR COLLEGE EXPERIENCE HANDBOOK

Character Development: Deepening the Significance of Learning

Letter to Self

This is a freestyle writing exercise. We have provided a few prompts to help you get started. Ask yourself: What do you want to say to yourself? Who are you? Who are you becoming? Are you proud of who you are becoming? Are you enjoying your accomplishments? What experiences have been life-changing or perspective-changing?

Date: _____

To: _____

_____
_____
_____
_____
_____
_____
_____
_____
_____
_____
_____
_____
_____
_____
_____
_____
_____
_____
_____
_____

Best Wishes

When you are done, share your letter with your Student Advocate or your classmates.

Academic Development: Meaning-Making

Chapter 7: Meaning Making

CCA Advisor Directions: This is the time in the semester when students tend to second guess their decision to attend college. Some students start to question their intellectual abilities. When doubt and uncertainty compete with focus and concentration, students find themselves looking for deeper reasons to continue through the semester. If ignored, these types of circumstances can spill over into students' attitude, perception, and worldview. Regardless of background, level of competency, or financial status, indefiniteness can be detrimental to academic pursuit and character development.

One way we have seen students respond positively to their concerns is by searching for a deeper connection with self. Meaning-making allows students to pinpoint their purpose in life, and they begin to understand that college is part of that development. Meaning-making helps you navigate campus and interact with others while you seek to understand your perception and response to your environment. Meaning-making will help you arrive at an understanding that adds value to your campus community.

First, discuss the following questions with your CCA and/or classmates. The answers to these questions will help you identify a greater purpose for wanting to excel in life and in the classroom. You will find this conversation rich and meaningful to your academic pursuit. Second, select two topics that influenced you the most and write a 250-word (max) essay.

Meaning-making	
Topic	Questions(s)
Hopes and Dreams	What do I want to do with my life? How do I find the intersection between my talents and my passions?
Values, Morals, Ethics	What do I really believe about right and wrong? What does it mean to live a good life?
Religion and Spirituality	What is the right religion for me? Why does God seem so far away from me on some days, and so close on others?
Core Relationships	Is there really a "soul mate" for me? Am I loveable?
Intersecting Identities	Who am I in relation to my skin color, social class, sexual orientation, religious background, and gender?
Education and Credentials	Is collegiality necessary for my future?
Career, Vocation, and Finances	How can I be sure that my future work will offer me the personal fulfillment of a vocation?
Civic Engagement	How do I pick my social issues? How can I fulfill my civic responsibility to improve the world locally, nationally, and internationally?
Wellness and Balance	How can I avoid burnout? Is multi-tasking the healthiest way to live a life?

CHAPTER 8

Applied Engaged Learning

This program inspired students by creating realistic, measurable steps for improvement and success. However, what impressed me most was the ease in which students were able to engage with and excel in diverse learning environments.

      Dr. Howard "H" Ward
      Assistant Vice President, Rochester Institute of Technology
      Dean of Students and Vice President of Student Affairs,
      Ohio Northern University, 1990 - 1996

                                      Components of this chapter was
                                      inspired by Marcia B. Baxter Magolda,
                        Elizabeth G. Creamer, and Peggy S. Meszaros

Character Development: Rewriting the Headlines

Over the next four years, there will be many headlines racing through your mind as you try to summarize the living-learning experience as an undergraduate student. The purpose of a headline is to indicate what follows it. Please keep in mind that the headline is supposed to quickly draw attention to the story, a story that can speak to your past, present, and future.

Imagine: What would the headline of your hometown local newspaper at your completion of year one be? In year two, what would be the headline of your article in the campus newspaper? In year three, what would be the headline in the New York Times about you? In your fourth year, what would be your headline in TIME magazine?

Discuss with your Student Advocate your rationale for selecting the headline. You can also share this information with your classmates. The job of the Student Advocate is to hold you accountable and motivate you to reach the goals you set in these headlines.

Year One:

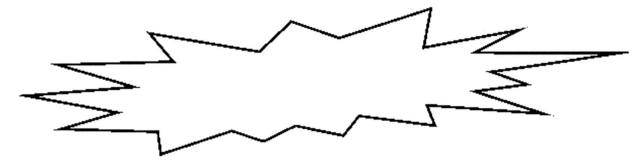

Year Two:

Year Three:

Year Four:

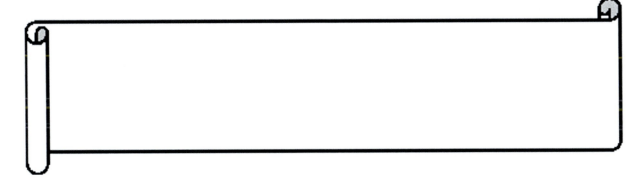

DEBRIEFING QUESTIONS:

- ☐ Are you on the right course?
- ☐ What will it take to achieve your goal?
- ☐ What resources do you need?
- ☐ What support do you need?
- ☐ What legacy do you want to leave?

Academic Development: Student Intelligence and Self-Authorship

Chapter 8: Advancing Academic and Social-Self Image through Self-Authorship

CCA Advisor Directions: One of the ways students can achieve the outcomes they desire is to understand that intelligence, wisdom, and experiences are assets to the learning environment. The power many students release once they arrive in college is the power of inner-voice. The classroom is a *mutual exchange, mutual benefit* zone. In other words, the classroom is a place for recognition of authoritative scholarship and constructive scholarship. Education is *not* meant to be top-down or bottom-up system. Education is circular; it integrates circles, colors, languages, reflections, reasoning, and ethics.

This unpopular perspective on education asks the student to take ownership over his or her beliefs, identities, and relationships and integrate them into the learning environment. Too often, students leave themselves at the door, and, as a result, the learning experience does not reach its full potential. How can students experience diverse ways of thinking if diversity never enters the classroom?

It is important that all students become authors of their own lives by shaping what they believe (epistemology), developing a sense of self (intrapersonal), and examining their relationship with others (interpersonal). This is a self-authorship exercise in which you will answer the questions below in journal form. We recommend you write 250-500 word entries for each section. When complete, discuss your journal entry with your CCA and classmates.

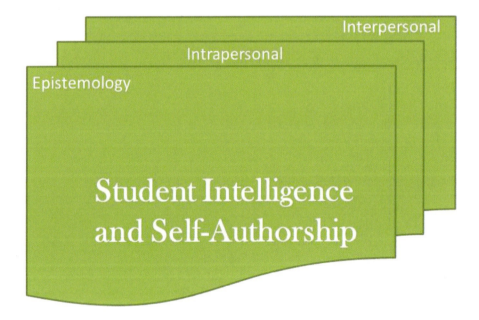

Journal Entry

1. **Epistemology** - As you reflect on your college experience, what do you believe is the single most important aspect of persevering to graduation? What knowledge have you gained from this experience? How are you sustaining this knowledge?

2. **Intrapersonal** - In what ways are you contributing to the conversation involving learning? What are you doing to ensure the success of others? How are you being helpful?

3. **Interpersonal** - How have you involved others in your learning? How is your learning impacting the lives of others?

Academic Development: Engaged Learning Differences

Chapter 8: Noteworthy "My"-stakes for Engaged Learners
CCA Advisor Directions: Students are constantly trying to take advantage of all college opportunities, but often they make decisions that hinder their progress towards excellence. One of the biggest "my"-stakes is when students think they already understand the campus culture; this may lead to a false sense of security when confronted with a challenge. Another "my"-stake is misinterpreting the value of the learning experience. Many students struggle for weeks or months before they figure out the value of navigating the campus culture.

An engaged learner understands the campus culture. Engaged learners are able to link learning with personal experiences to achieve success. Engaged learners learn best from their own experiences by transferring outside knowledge into the classroom to solve problems in both settings. Most importantly, engaged learners work collaboratively with others because they recognize the potential in others.

Group Reflection Paper

Three to five (3-5) students will be assigned to a group to write a reflection paper on Engaged Learning. In the paper, the group will reflect on the importance of linking personal experiences to learning. Some groups may feel opposed to such a notion, while others are in favor of the position. Opposing views are welcome in the paper. Use the criteria below to construct your paper.

1) Assign duties and tasks (who will research, type, etc…)
2) Supporting evidence must be clearly stated and supported.
3) The narrative must be 5-7 pages in length.
4) The paper must be peer reviewed.

Components of the Reflection Paper

- ☐ Introduction
- ☐ Position on Engaged Learning
- ☐ Brief Literature Review
- ☐ Closing Position
- ☐ Summary
- ☐ References

CHAPTER 9

Assessing the "Living-Learning" Experience

"When I started college, I underestimated the importance of building relationships. This program provided a framework to engage my professors as equals and develop long term relationships. Meanwhile, the exercises and meetings helped me understand how I work best in new settings. The same exercises and strategies have helped me now as a young adult and as a young professional."

> Tyrice Johnson,
> Cloud CRM Sales Consultant, Oracle
> Elon University, 2009 – 2013

Components of this chapter was inspired by Edward T. Hall

ASSESSING THE "LIVING-LEARNING" EXPERIENCE

Character Development: It Takes a Village

At this point in the semester, it has become apparent that peer support is an essential part of the first-year experience. You have learned to rely on and trust the support of your suitemates or classmates. Their thoughts and opinions have influenced you greatly. Another layer of support has come from faculty, staff, and support staff. These professionals have made lasting impressions on you. These individuals are now your teachers, educators, role models, and surrogate parents. Collectively, there are many people responsible for your growth and development. It is important that you recognize the communal support you have received thus far and acknowledge the firm hands that have shaped your thoughts and behavior.

Thought Letter

This exercise is a one-to-two page exploratory writing assignment that focuses on one particular thought you would like your readers to know. This is not a formal letter, so it is not bound to the limits of organization, style, or references. The Thought Letter is a way to observe the writer's thinking process. Please remember you are writing to an entire group.

> *Dear Friends*
>
> *It is with great excitement that I write this letter. You have been such an inspiration to me.*

Academic Development: Meaningful Relationships

Chapter 9: Meaningful Relationships

CCA Advisor Directions: As students approach the remaining weeks in first semester, it is important that they differentiate academic, personal, social, and public space. These spaces support and protect students' mental and emotional health, including the ability to make good decisions. Although the diagram shows different degrees of spatial order, all spaces deserve equal attention and maintenance.

Your academic space is your most prized possession. Academic space can be defined as the capacity to retain and regurgitate information. Personal space can be defined as the space that people are permitted to enter and exit in relationship. Social space is the unguarded space that all must intentionally enter into. Public space is shared space.

This 30,000 ft., eagle-eye view gives you a visual of the potential impact nonacademic spaces can have on your learning. As you know, these spaces can produce positive and negative results. Your relationships in these spaces play a major role in the results you want for your academic success.

In the space provided, name the people who have contributed significantly to your academic success. Then, indicate what attributes they bring to the table. Third, decide if these individuals represent primary or secondary links to your academic space.

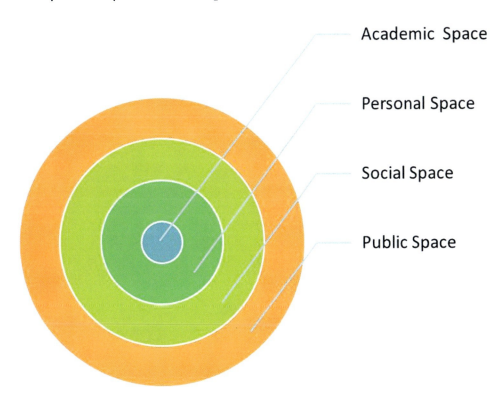

Adopted and modified from Edward T. Hall's personal reaction bubbles.

ASSESSING THE "LIVING-LEARNING" EXPERIENCE

Space	People	Attributes	Primary/Secondary Link

1. Which attributes are most likely to complement you?

2. Which attributes are least likely to complement you?

Special Note: Please remember to revisit your Academic Goals sheet.

CHAPTER 10

New Environments Call for New Perspectives

"This program motivated me to not only attain my undergraduate degree but also earn my graduate degree. This program instilled discipline in areas needing development."

> Mohamadou Souleymane Diallo,
> Area Credit Manager, Gexpro
> Buena Vista University, 1998 - 2002

> NEW ENVIRONMENTS CALL FOR NEW PERSPECTIVES

Character Development: Journey Walk

There are critical times in the semester when students need to pause and reflect on personal growth and development in the first-year college experience. There are also times when students are dealing with traumatic experiences that are beyond their control. A Journey Walk is a time to reconnect with what matters. Students have raved about this exercise because it helped them examine their life without feedback, criticism, or interruption.

The Journey Walk is a silent exercise that can be facilitated using different strategies; pick the strategy below that best addresses individual needs or the needs of your cohort, group, or class. These combinations have served students well. Feel free to customize your own Journey Walk. *For best results, facilitate this exercise in the early evening when the sun is setting or at night when the stars are shining.*

Journey Walk A

Facilitator(s):

1. Pick a space in the room.
2. For 5 minutes, try not to think about anything.
3. Then, think about the people around you (3 minutes).
4. Think about how all of you are connected (3 minutes).
5. Think about what you have accomplished this semester (3 minutes).
6. Take a walk by yourself and reflect on your thoughts (10 minutes).
7. When students return, discuss thoughts, emotions, and reactions as a group.

Journey Walk B

Facilitator(s):

1. Lie on the ground and look at the stars.
2. For 5 minutes, try not to think about anything.
3. Think about someone close to you who is in pain (3 minutes).
4. Think about how they are handling the pain (3 minutes).
5. Think about how you are handling their pain (3 minutes).
6. Take a walk with a partner, and, if you are comfortable, share your thoughts and emotions with your partner (10 minutes).
7. When students return, discuss as a group one thing each person wants for the person in pain.

HELPFUL TIPS:
1. Make sure you have the counselor-on-call contact information or invite them to attend the exercise.
2. Inform students that they can stop the exercise at any moment.
3. Alternatively, students can write their feelings in a journal.
4. The facilitator is the first to arrive and last to leave. Be vigilant with follow up to students.

THE FIRST-YEAR COLLEGE EXPERIENCE HANDBOOK

Academic Development: Academic Wellness

Chapter 10: Academic Wellness

CCA Advisor Directions: Students often enter college underestimating the rigorous demands for meeting deadlines, preparing for final exams, or completing group projects. Heading into the final weeks of the semester, students may have decided to generate to-do lists in order to be more effective and efficient with their limited time. In most cases, this method has proven advantageous for students, but some students do not benefit from it.

There are several educational values that play a major role in students' academic development: time management, social involvement, classroom preparation, study habits, reading and writing skills, test preparation skills, feelings about learning, values, and goals. These educational values are important aspects for properly preparing for the end of the semester.

Below are eight (8) educational values. Please take a few minutes to place an "x" next to the statements that best describe your learning experience. Then draw your attention back to the diagram and draw connections between the educational values. For example, if you place an "x" next to "I am very excited about final exams" under Feelings About Learning, show how this impacts other values, such as Classroom Preparation.

Special Note: The objective is to draw a correlation between educational values.

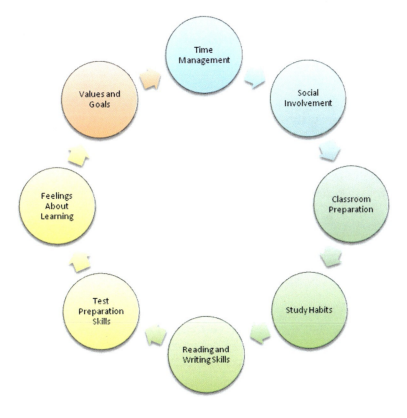

NEW ENVIRONMENTS CALL FOR NEW PERSPECTIVES

Time Management:
- ___ I am able to make the necessary plans to be effective and efficient in the classroom.
- ___ I plan to study 4-6 hours a day and 35-40 hours a week in preparation for final exams.
- ___ I will complete all assignments leading to final exams.
- ___ I procrastinate on a regular basis.

Social Involvement:
- ___ I am able to say "No" to social events that disrupt my studies.
- ___ My friends are serious about their studies.
- ___ Studying is more important that socializing.
- ___ I am over-involved in my student organization(s).

Classroom Preparation:
- ___ I attend all my classes with regularity.
- ___ I visit with my academic advisor when necessary.
- ___ I complete my assignments 3-5 days in advance.
- ___ I review my notes before class.
- ___ I have no idea what is going on in class before I arrive.

Study Habits:
- ___ I study at a scheduled time each day.
- ___ I am more effective and efficient when studying alone.
- ___ I use my calendar/planner effectively and efficiently.
- ___ I plan well, but I do not execute my plan very well.

Reading and Writing Skills:
- ___ My long papers have 1-2 drafts before submission.
- ___ I enjoy reading before class.
- ___ I visit the Writing Center before I submit my paper.
- ___ I enjoy reading my notes before and after class.
- ___ I dislike reading, so I skim paragraphs.

Test Preparation Skills:
- ___ I am very organized for my tests, major projects, and presentations.
- ___ I usually study exactly what is on the tests.
- ___ I start studying for tests one week in advance.
- ___ I only study the night before the test.

Feelings About Learning:
- ___ I am very excited about final exams.
- ___ I enjoy learning and look forward to challenges in the classroom.
- ___ I enjoy 2-3 of my classes the most.
- ___ I enjoy college but not homework, test, etc.

Values and Goals:
- ___ I have reached my goals for the semester.
- ___ I have not worked hard this semester.
- ___ The habits I am acquiring will benefit my professional development immensely.
- ___ A college education is essential to my personal growth and development.

What new realities have you discovered about your learning experience? Describe the relationships between your educational values.

Example: My <u>feelings about learning</u> impact <u>my study habits</u>.

Educational Value	Attitude and Perception	Educational Value	Learning Outcomes (What will you be able to do? What impact will this have on your learning?)
Feeling About Learning	I am very excited about final exams.	Study Habits	I will devote the necessary hours in advance to prepare for finals.

CHAPTER 11

Do More by Doing Less

"One of the keys to academic success is identifying your strengths and weaknesses as a student. This is important because it helps you transform into the person and leader, you never imagined being. This program helped me carve out the time to create a plan for academic and social success."

    Johnessia Thomas,
    Senior Social Worker II, Truman Medical Center
    Buena Vista University, 200 - 2006

Character Development: Emulating Success

Chapter 11: Emulating Success
CCA Advisor Directions: What does success look like? What does success sound like? Where does success experience its greatest achievements? How does success walk? Where does success go after success? By this point in the semester, students have learned that there are varying degrees of success.

How do you define success? What are the examples of success? Take a few minutes to brainstorm a few examples of social success. Then, conduct an interview with a fellow student inquiring about the level of responsibility to self, campus involvement, and moral position on character.

Interview Questions

Briefly, tell me about your achievements in and outside of the classroom this semester.
_____
_____

Please describe the achievement that has had the greatest influence on your life.
_____
_____

Describe a person you see as successful.
_____
_____

How have you learned to build your social network?
_____
_____

Which of your character traits have been most effective in your college environment?
_____
_____

How do you know you are successful?
_____
_____

What are the qualities of good character?
_____
_____

DO MORE BY DOING LESS

What does your responsibility to mentor others entail?
_____
_____

Why should companies hire you post-graduation?
_____
_____

If you were not in college right now, what would you be doing?
_____
_____

Academic Development: Efficiency and Effectiveness

<u>**Chapter 11: From Social Development to Career Development**</u>
<u>**CCA Directions:**</u>
Efficiency = students' use of time, effort and quality
Effective= doing a job/task well enough to reach the intended outcome (ex: studying to get an A, outcome = A =effective).

The purpose of this activity is to gauge students' sense of efficiency and effectiveness. This exercise will reveal the disparity (if any) between specific skills (ex: 90% in time management efficiency but 75% efficiency in meeting deadlines). Help students understand why disparities exist: "What habits and practices are at play to perpetuate these scores?" and, "What habits and behavior changes can help the student improve?"

Exercise:
Go through each skill and rate efficiency and effectiveness (it may help to think in terms of letter grades. Example: Time Management 92% in Efficiency=A and 76% in Effectiveness=C). Discuss the scores and disparities in each graph and between graphs (e.g., discuss the score for time management in the Efficiency graph vs Effective graph).

<u>**Mastering Effectiveness and Efficiency**</u>

How can you be an Effective and Efficient student?

One writer noted people who climb to the top of their field eclipse their peers through one basic concept: *deliberate practice.* The writer said the practice doesn't make perfect, but *perfect practice* makes *perfect.* Strategy 9 focuses on enhancing your skills through deliberate, perfect practice.

You have arrived at the point of the program where your success is somewhere between good and perfect. Success is effort, commitment, and triumph. In order to move from a possible state of being to present realization, or from *chance* to *deliberate*, you must turn your full attention to being effective and efficient. One strategy for being more deliberate in effectiveness and efficiency is to identify when you disengage, daydream, procrastinate, and withdraw.

Another task of deliberate practice is to establish mini goals. This may include timed studying, change of eating habits, or monitoring and recording success and failure. Surprisingly, documenting failure is one of the most effective ways to prepare for setbacks and to build resilience. Another way to think about failure is to see setbacks and/or disempowered failure as commas rather than periods in your learning experience. We encourage you to keep learning after each comma.

DO MORE BY DOING LESS

Efficiency vs. Effectiveness

Efficiency					
	100-90%	89-80%	79-70%	69-60%	59% & Below
Time Management					
Planning					
Setting Priorities					
Organization					
Studying					
Meeting Deadlines					

*Efficiency can be defined as spending less time, less effort, less money, etc., while still doing a job well. Maximize output with minimum input.

Effectiveness					
	100-90%	89-80%	79-70%	69-60%	59% & Below
Time Management					
Planning					
Setting Priorities					
Organization					
Studying					
Meeting Deadlines					

*Effectiveness can be defined as doing your job well—performing with quality and producing results. Does the actual output meet the desired output?

THE FIRST-YEAR COLLEGE EXPERIENCE HANDBOOK

Attention All Students!

At this point, we encourage you to examine all you are involved with and start to scale back on your commitments. We are not asking you to drop or quit student organizations or withdraw from other responsibilities that are non-academic; only lessen your commitment to each organization. The concept of "Do More By Doing Less" allows you to be **_more_** effective and efficient in your commitments by doing **_less._**

College life is a very exciting and complicated transition in your life. You are surrounded by so many different and wonderful opportunities. As you approach final exams, projects, and presentations, allow yourself time to be successful. Talk to your student organization leaders about effective ways to minimize your role in the organization in order to also perform sufficiently in the classroom. This may also mean you consider not traveling home, minimizing social events and activities, and monitoring interactive media sources for at least the few weeks leading up to finals.

As students are fighting to meet the academic demands on their life to complete the semester in victory, they lose sight of themselves; as a result, fatigue, exhaustion, and stress begin to influence mind, body, and soul. At times, as levels of concentration increase, so does anxiety. Students push and press through the rigor of projects, papers, and exams to meet the academic expectations of the institution.

However, these are also times when the body begins to breakdown. The love and need for success mentally and emotional tears down the body, which ultimately causes great harm to the physical body. Students tend to experience severe bouts of various sicknesses due to the overwhelming commitments to their curricular and co-curricular involvement. Some of these symptoms/illnesses include:

1. Cold
2. Flu
3. Stomach Pain
4. Nervousness
5. Jitters
6. Vomiting
7. Headaches
8. Dizziness
9. Numbness

These are often caused by procrastination, late nights, stress, anxiety, over commitment, peer pressure, unhealthy relationships, poor dieting, and fear of failure. Be careful about your level of commitment as you approach the last 2-3 weeks of the semester.

Debriefing:
1. **What are you willing to let go?**
2. **How are your commitments impacting your health?**
3. **What support are you receiving from family, friends, faculty, and/or staff?**
4. **How are you treating your condition?**

Part 4: Transformative Knowledge

The knowledge contained in this text is designed as a guide first-year students' transition to college.

It is our hope that this text speaks to the heart and soul of education: You, the learner! This text's intent is to help students climb the ranks of education by qualifying them as rigorous learners.

In order to inspire you to continue in your transformative experience (your life-long journey), we selected the butterfly to help you understand that every phase of your development matters. The finished product also matters! Graduation matters! But do not take for granted the steps along the way. Transformation also Matters!

CHAPTER 12

Social Intelligence

"It's a relief that there is an academic program designed to relate to your situation: a program that can facilitate your growth as well as inspire you to perform at the highest level."

>Rev. Terrell "Redd" Reddix
>Teacher, Athletic Director, Ginn Academy
>Pastor, Greater Works Church of God in Christ
>Ohio Northern University, 1992 – 1997
>Mechanical Engineering

Character Development: "A Piece of the Puzzle"

Is it fair to say that you have not yet reached your full potential? Is it safe to say: who you are today is not fully who you aspire to be? Students have passionately expressed the idea that what others see in them is just a piece of the puzzle! Some of you have suppressed your feelings to avoid conflict or walked away from difficult situations. By not expressing your feelings to some degree, you have hindered your growth and development. We realize some would argue that avoiding conflict for the betterment of the campus community is a good thing. However, many students who suppress their true feelings end up surrendering to frustration and cynicism.

You may pretend all is well. You may wear the mask to avoid being characterized as "that girl" or "that guy." You smile, cheer, and advocate for others to demonstrate outward affection, while you are actually doing so to guard your true emotions. You think you can't be your authentic self because you assume your circle of influence is not prepared to receive the true you!

The nature of the problem is that students who sacrifice acting according to their authentic selves to avoid conflict rarely reach their full potential in the classroom. In order to experience true success in the classroom without emotional reservations, you must "put all the pieces on the table." This will help you visualize how beautiful and wonderful, yet complicated and difficult, you are. Your diversity is important to your campus!

Use the large puzzle below to write about five (5) situations or events that summarize your academic and social experience. You should concentrate on two aspects of life and write one word for each aspect: 1) emotion (positive or negative) and 2) setting (where were you on campus or in the community). Do not record what happened; simply write the emotion and setting. Discuss the following with your Student Advocate:

1. What triggered the emotion?
2. Who witnessed this situation?
3. Was your reaction positive or negative?
4. As a result of your decision to act or not to act, what were your feelings when you walked away?
5. Do you feel proud of your decision?
6. Are you upset about your decision?

In which setting would you like to respond differently in the future? Write the emotion and setting in the red puzzle piece. Why do you want to respond differently?

SOCIAL INTELLIGENCE

Character Development: Managing the Mask

Chapter 12: Managing the Mask
CCA Directions: Now that students have a deeper understanding of college life (i.e., how it feels to meet deadlines, take tests, participate in group projects, and talk with faculty), let's talk about how students manage their emotions. Managing stress effectively is the key to finishing the semester in good standing. Too often, students ignore their emotions by focusing on the finish line. The problem is that when students neglect their emotions the finish line moves further into the distance. Over time, students become emotionally fatigued, which prevents them from performing at the highest level of achievement.

This exercise is designed to help students succeed emotionally, which is paramount to their academic success. In order for students to manage their emotions, they must be in tune with how they are feeling. No study skill is effective if a student is too anxious to remember the material or has a panic attack during an exam.

In this exercise, check the emotion(s) you experience in a given week or day. Discuss your emotion(s) with your Student Advocate. The focus of the conversation should involve what the triggers of that emotion are (e.g., anxiety: I have always done poorly at the end of the semester, so I am anxious that the pattern will repeat itself).

Emotional Intelligence

___Valued	___Hatred	___Intelligent	___Revengeful	___Angry
___Embarrassed	___Blame	___Inspired	___Sad	___Tense
___Irritated	___Exhausted	___Afraid	___Bitter	___Guilty
___Alone	___Joyful	___Loveless	___Shocked	___Ignored
___Connected	___Uncomfortable	___Depressed	___Irresponsible	___Failure
___Regretful	___Responsible	___Frustrated	___Courageous	___Champion
___Confused	___Lost	___Unprepared	___Miserable	___Happy
___Isolated	___Comfortable	___Shameful	___Confident	___Secure
___Happy	___Proud	___Dignified	___Scholarly	___Relieved
___Capable	___Worthy	___Respected	___Confident	___Comfortable

If you feel comfortable doing so, share your experience with other students and your Student Advocate. If there are feelings or emotional charges you are experiencing that are not listed above, please feel free to write those feelings below. The purpose of this exercise is to successfully and consistently monitor your emotions throughout the program.

SOCIAL INTELLIGENCE

Character Development: Social Situational Awareness

Chapter 12: Social Situational Awareness
CCA Directions: Now that students are gearing up for final exams, they probably have noticed a sudden shift in the campus culture. The study lounges are filled to capacity, there are no available seats in the library, and the residence halls are quiet. This cultural shift can seem awkward, but it is real! Students have a tendency to focus more as the semester comes to a close.

It is important to step away from homework and meetings briefly to observe the cultural shift taking place before your eyes. As your peers panic to complete assignments in a timely manner or rush to the library to print a paper, you will find yourself embracing or rejecting this behavior.

In small groups or with your cohort, discuss your reaction to the questions below. Discuss your responses with your Student Advocate.

Group Discussion

1) What have you learned about the academic and social culture of the university this last semester?

2) As you approach the end of the semester, what campus climate changes have you noticed? (i.e., study habits, student gathering spaces, etc.)

3) Have you observed any adjustments in student study habits in preparation for finals? (i.e., number of hours of study, location of study)

4) What mood changes have you observed in the campus community in recent days?

5) What strategies are you planning to use in preparation for finals?

6) How has your perspective on learning changed?

SOCIAL INTELLIGENCE

Academic Development: Academic Situational Awareness

Chapter 12: Academic Situational Awareness
CCA Directions: Similar to Social Situational Awareness, Academic Situational Awareness notates the critical elements of the syllabus that require immediate attention leading into final exams. If students pay close attention to syllabi, they will find more demands or emphasis on tests, projects, homework, presentations, and papers while also preparing for finals.

Don't panic. It's not going away, so develop a plan. The best way to approach the last few weeks of the semester is to develop a three-week plan. It is important you realize that there is very little room for error. In other words, you are competing with the last three weeks of the semester. Your three-week plan has to be clear and concise.

To execute your three-week plan effectively, you need a different level of concentration. For some, the final three weeks of the semester can improve, sustain, or reduce your academic status. If you haven't already done so, review your syllabus and calculate your standing in the course.

Keep your syllabus handy; you will use it to complete the activity sheet below. If the information needed is not provided on the syllabus, please solicit the assistance of your professor.

Three-Week Goal

Course	Existing Grade/ Expected Grade	Presentation	Project/ Group Project	Paper	Final Exam	Due Date

THREE-WEEK PLAN

Goals (Improve or sustain)	Tasks (Homework, Papers, Projects, etc.)	Wanted Outcome	Strategies (What do you need to do?)	Assessment	Results
To sustain my current "A" in Biology	2 Papers	To achieve 90% or better on each assignment	Complete rough draft early to submit to Writing Center	Submit paper to Writing Center two weeks before due date	

CHAPTER 13

Bias in the Face of Diversity

"This program, formerly the Academic Enrichment Program, provided me with a knowledgeable mentor and guide. Having an on-campus resource to help me and check in with my progress truly helped me with the adjustment from high school to college. I gained a better understanding of what Elon offers and valuable information on resources that will benefit my college success."

    Katrina Clifford,
    Environmental Studies
    Elon University, Class of 2017

Components of the chapter was inspired by Claude M. Steele

Character Development: Identity Development and Critical Thinking

One of the things the authors of this text have in common is a passion for diversity and multiculturalism. There are two primary principles that have guided much of our discussion related to diversity: tolerance and inclusivity. In many respects, tolerance and inclusivity have lifted the burden of despair and made very complex situations simple.

As a first-year student, you have probably attended a diversity program that focused on race, gender, religion, sexual orientation, and class. Traditionally, these types of programs have challenged audiences to accept the responsibility of addressing acts of hate. We recognize the responsibility to eradicate hate should not fall on the shoulders of only one person. In fact, eradicating hate should be the responsibility of the entire campus. Unfortunately, many students leave the room disempowered because they feel overwhelmed at the idea that they must enact change alone.

Students are too often asked to lead these discussions without formal training and education. Students are thrown into these discussions unsure of their own position on diversity. As you observe your campus, you will wrestle with emotions that push you in the direction of advocate or bystander, but you must be allowed to get there over time.

First-year students are unaware that their position on diversity has a lot to do with their identity. The concept of identity challenges campuses to continue the conversation about race. The same is true for religion or interfaith.

Identity is a necessary conversation on all college campuses. When students discuss their identity in relation to race, and religion, relationships between students and with the campus community deepen. Specifically, discussion on identity allows students to more successfully engage with the campus community.

Group exercise.

Please select three questions from the list of open-ended questions below. Your group must propose and justify its answers. Please summarize your group's answer to each question in one sentence. This sentence serves as the group's thesis statement. Choose someone in the group to present the group's position and defense on the subject.

BIAS IN THE FACE OF DIVERSITY

QUESTIONS

1. How is your identity celebrated on campus?
2. What impact does your perspective on your identity have on your learning?
3. Describe a time when you were uncomfortable with a class assignment.
4. How does your learning environment complement your learning style?
5. How has the first-year experience influenced your ability to interact with others?
6. How has the first-year experience influenced your perspective on the campus community?
7. What is hindering you from maximizing your potential in the classroom?
8. How has your identity impacted your contribution to group projects?

THE FIRST-YEAR COLLEGE EXPERIENCE HANDBOOK

Academic Development: Transformative Experience

Chapter 13: "What's Hindering My Transformative Experience?"
CCA Advisor Directions: We highly value the totality of the learning experience, and no transformative experience exists without careful consideration of all aspects of the first-year experience. With this in mind, ask students to share thoughts or experiences that may be hindering their progress in the classroom. More importantly, ask students to share any apprehensions that may be influencing their ability to focus on their finals.

Some distractions are non-threatening. However, there are occasions when certain distractions are more threatening than others. This exercise will provide students with the opportunity to share their view of the campus climate. Transformative knowledge cannot occur in an environment fostering oppression.

It is important that first-year students recognize instances of micro-aggression and micro-insults that impact their transformative experience. Below, place an "X" in the space provided that explains an experience you had during the fall semester. This information will help you discuss incidents openly. More importantly, this exercise provides an opportunity to seek help before entering into final exams.

Microaggressions are "brief and commonplace daily verbal, behavioral, and environmental indignities, whether intentional or unintentional, that communicate hostile, derogatory or negative racial [discriminatory] slights and insults that potentially have harmful or unpleasant psychological impact on the target person or group." (Solorzano, Ceja, & Yosso, 2000)

Microinsults are behaviors, actions, or verbal remarks that convey rudeness, insensitivity, or demean a person's group, or social identity, or heritage. (Sue, et al. 2007)

_____ Continued mispronunciation of the names of students after corrected many times:
   "Is Jose Cuinantile here?" "I am here, but my name is Jesus Quintanilla."

_____ Tests and project due dates scheduled on religious or cultural holidays:
   "It has been pointed out that I scheduled the mid-term during Rosh Hashanah."

_____ Low expectations set for students from historically low-performing groups or high schools:
   "Oh, Robert, you're from the local public school? You are going to need lots of academic help."

_____ Mainstream students validated and historically marginalized students ignored during class discussion:
   "Let's call on John again. He has great experiences and responses to some of these problems."

_____ Inappropriate humor in class or residence hall that degrades students from different groups:
   "Anyone want to hear a good joke? Ok, There was a Jew, a Mexican, and a Black…"

_____ Discussions of racially charged political opinions in class while targets of those opinions are assumed to be absent from class roster:
   "I think illegal aliens are criminals because they are breaking the law and need to be rounded up and sent back to Mexico."

BIAS IN THE FACE OF DIVERSITY

_____ Debates in class or residence halls that place students from minority groups in a difficult position:
"Today we are going to have a debate on immigration. I expect there will be opposing views on the subject based on the ethnicity/race variation in the room."

_____ Students' experiences discredited or denied by questioning the credibility of their stories:
"That is not true for all African Americans. That must just be your experience."

_____ Use of heterosexist examples or sexist language in class:
"For the class project, I want you to think about a romantic relationship that you have had with a member of the opposite sex."

_____ Class projects assigned that ignore differences in socioeconomic class status:
"For this class, you are required to visit four art galleries located in the downtown area. The entrance fee for each is $10.

_____ Students singled out in class because of unique backgrounds:
"You're an international student; can you share with us what it is like for you to live in America?"

_____ US citizenship and full comprehension of English language and US culture assumed:
"What do you mean you never heard of the Bill Cosby? Have you been living under a rock?"

_____ Students discouraged from working on projects that explore their own social identities:
"If you are Native American, I don't want you to write your paper on Native Americans. Try something different."

Debriefing:

1) In what ways have these experiences impacted your learning?

2) Have you shared this information with others? If so, whom and why?

3) Are you receiving the help you need to make healthy decisions?

4) Are you familiar with the campus resources available on campus? If not, please seek assistance.

THE FIRST-YEAR COLLEGE EXPERIENCE HANDBOOK

Academic Development: Stereotype Threat

Chapter 13: Stereotype Threat Is Real
CCA Advisor Directions: For the last two decades, we have worked in educational settings designed to empower students to accept the challenge of learning in environments slightly different from what they are used to. These settings have empowered some and tested others. The student experience has taught us that the greatest challenge facing first-year students is the setting itself. We have learned through our own academic advising experience that these settings are full of joy, pain, pleasantries, and shame. Regardless of whether it's a student's first time on campus, his or her first semester, or first final exam, college can be intimidating.

This chapter focuses on helping students understand *stereotype threat*. Specifically, this exercise will help you process any apprehensions you may be experiencing in preparing for final exams. More importantly, this approach will allow you to make the necessary adjustment prior to final exams. Ultimately, we want you to enter second semester with a greater understanding of your learning environment.

Your Personal Journal

Choose 2-3 topics and answer the questions accordingly. For each entry, write 250 words or less.

CLASSROOM SETTING
1) When you walked into the classroom for the first time, what was your perception?
2) How did you handle the anxiety?
3) What was your greatest concern when walking in the classroom?
4) What strategies did you use to embrace the challenge?
5) How would you rate your reaction to the class on a scale of 1 to 5, with 5 being excellent?
6) Which of your reaction behaviors are you willing to accept? Which would you like to discard?

PROFESSOR INTERACTION
1) When you approached your professor for the first time, what was your perception?
2) How did you handle the anxiety?
3) What was your greatest concern when approaching the professor?
4) What strategies did you use to embrace the challenge?
5) How would you rate your reaction to the opportunity on a scale of 1 to 5, with 5 being excellent?
6) Which of your reaction behaviors are you willing to accept? Which would you like to discard?

TEST & QUIZZES
1) When you sat down to take a test for the first time, what was your perception?
2) How did you handle the anxiety?
3) What was your greatest concern when taking the test?
4) What strategies did you use to embrace the challenge?
5) How would you rate your reaction to the test on a scale of 1 to 5, with 5 being excellent?
6) Which of your reaction behaviors are you willing to accept? Which would you like to discard?

BIAS IN THE FACE OF DIVERSITY

PRESENTATIONS
1) When you walked in the front of the class for the first time, what was your perception?
2) How did you handle the anxiety?
3) What was your greatest concern when going in front of the classroom?
4) What strategies did you use to embrace the challenge?
5) How would you rate your reaction to the presentation on a scale of 1 to 5, with 5 being excellent?
6) Which of your reaction behaviors are you willing to accept? Which would you like to discard?

Summary:

What have you learned about yourself from this exercise?

What realities are you willing to accept or reject?

CHAPTER 14

Intellectual Diversity

"This program helped me understand the intrinsic value of education. Specifically, this program challenged me to appreciate and compete with my peers on a daily basis."

    Kenny Muldrow,
    Carl Buddig & Company, IT Support Technician
    Buena Vista University, 2006 - 2010

Components of this chapter was inspired by Elizabeth F. Barkley

INTELLECTUAL DIVERSITY

Character Development: Crossing the Finish Line

You have almost reached the end of the semester. The fact that you have reached this point is an accomplishment worth celebrating. Take a minute to reflect on your experience. Your accomplishments this semester are remarkable. You have learned to manage your independence. You need very little instruction in the classroom, supervision on the job, or direction making healthy decisions.

You have reached a milestone. Don't minimize your success. The knowledge and skills gained have helped you learn to prioritize, plan ahead, make connections, problem solve, and know yourself. Be proud of your success, but don't be complacent. You must finish the race.

After a long, hard-fought semester, you realize you are approaching the finish line. The distance between you and the finish line requires concentration and discipline. No matter what your goals were this semester, crossing the finish line is important. It doesn't matter if you finish standing or flat on your back. Just finish!

Finish Line

1) **Choose one idea that will help you cross the finish line.**
2) **Write two or three questions about the idea.**
3) **Write a short answer to each question.**
4) **Discuss your answers with your Student Advocate.**

Academic Development: Erasing Doubt

Chapter 14: Erasing Doubt
CCA Advisor Directions: One of the most rewarding aspects of the first-year experience is the knowledge students gain of themselves. As first-year students begin to reflect on their first semester, they are often examining their personal growth and development. Many realize that college has presented academic and social challenges. Regardless of personal success or failure, most students are willing to strengthen their identity and character by avoiding assimilation. True diversity is allowing the uniqueness of every individual and affinity group the opportunity to sustain itself. This is not possible via assimilation. We have seen students perform better in the classroom and live with a greater sense of purpose when they have a greater understanding of who they are. Students who are self-aware have a greater probability of success in the classroom and are consciously active participants of the campus community.

In this exercise, draw from personal experiences to finish the semester proud of who you are and what you accomplished. This is an important phase of development entering final exams because it provides confidence, comfort, and support of self.

STUDY HABITS

____   I know my strengths and underdevelopments.

____   I am self-motivated, so I study alone.

____   I love studying with others; other people motivate me.

____   I know I have made significant strides in my effort to achieve my academic goals.

STUDENT ENGAGEMENT

____   I know my limitations and boundaries.

____   I have made an informed decision to refrain from all student organization or affinity group activities.

____   I have friends who want the best for me.

____   I love being involved in student organizations and have found balance between them and academics.

MOTIVATION

____   I am inspired to finish the semester with a positive attitude.

____   I am confident that I can perform in my final exams.

____   I will not allow my surroundings to dictate my enthusiasm.

____   I am excited to compete with my peers.

INTELLECTUAL DIVERSITY

EXPECTANCY

___ I expect a lot from myself.

___ I will do my best.

___ I know what success feels like, and I want that feeling again.

___ I set the bar, so I can also raise the bar.

INTEGRITY

___ I will invest in the academic outcomes I desire.

___ I will be disciplined in my studies.

___ I am the only person responsible for my personal success.

___ I will designate time to study in academic settings.

VALUE

___ I have a clear picture of how I am approaching final exams.

___ I respect the effort and hard work I have put in this semester.

___ I understand that expectancy and value are co-dependent.

___ I love the academic challenge that stands before me.

GOAL SETTING

___ I know exactly what I need to do in order to reach my goals for the semester.

___ I have goals that are still attainable.

___ I have personal goals and academic goals.

___ I will achieve my goals if I stay committed to my plan.

This was adopted and modified from Elizabeth F. Barkley, *Student Engagement Techniques: A handbook for College Faculty*. (San Francisco, CA, Jossey-Bass, 2010.)

CHAPTER 15

Diversity Intelligence Matters

"Looking back on my college years, I realized that one of the key initiatives was the academic awareness program in the Multicultural Center. This program not only stressed the importance of education but also the importance of casting a wide net for personal growth and development."

> Lou Averhart
> Quality Leader, GE Aviation-Durham
>
> Ohio Northern University
> Mechanical Engineering, 1994 - 1998

Components of this chapter was
inspired by James A. Anderson

DIVERSITY INTELLIGENCE MATTERS

Character Development: The Significance of Diverse Thinking

SELF ASSESSMENT

One of the many challenges facing college campuses is the task of facilitating difficult dialogues related to diversity. College campuses make every attempt to create initiatives that help to embrace diversity, multiculturalism, inclusivity, and pluralism, while confronting biases, stereotypes, preconceived notions, discrimination, threats, and racism. Diversity and multicultural topics have a tendency to challenge college campuses to engage in a dialogue that may not be suited for their constituents (faculty, staff, and students) and stakeholders (trustees). Though challenging, these conversations are necessary.

What makes a dialogue difficult? What makes diversity a difficult dialogue? Diversity and multiculturalism are not difficult dialogues at all. What is difficult is being honest. We all have a tendency to avoid conversations that may trigger hopelessness, anxiety, and anger. We protect others by protecting ourselves. Many of us believe our truth will hurt us and cause hurt, so it is best that we don't say anything.

Though this may be true, it is the opposite of what is needed to create a learning environment conducive to different learning styles and lifestyles. In other words, diverse thinking and experiences become lost in the conversation because we have conditioned ourselves to disengage with or withdraw from the conversation. If everyone in the classroom is takes the same approach, we are left with a room of silence. Moreover, very few people in the room are skilled in facilitating these moments of silence.

We recognize that this topic deserves more attention. The exercise below serves as a jumping-off point for first-year students, Student Advocates, and Co-Curricular Advisors. This exercise best fits a group, cohort, or classroom setting because it is in these settings that every student is allowed to be transparent and vulnerable. We have also provided some rules that may be helpful to the conversation.

RULES

- ☐ Nothing is to be taken personally.
- ☐ No comment will be ignored.
- ☐ Be present in the conversation to support others.
- ☐ Everyone must participate.
- ☐ This is a non-judgment zone.
- ☐ Everyone is to be respected.
- ☐ Don't dismiss what is being said by anyone.
- ☐ Don't let the seriousness of the conversation stop you from participating.
- ☐ Learn something.

THE FIRST-YEAR COLLEGE EXPERIENCE HANDBOOK

Place a check mark (√) in front of the items that best describe you and your experience. Immediately following this exercise, discuss the items you checked with your Student Advocate and Co-Curricular Advisor and decide which steps to take next.

___ I have to act differently in class than I do outside of class.

___ I have to pause before I speak in class.

___ I have to code switch when I am away from my affinity group.

___ I smile when I don't want to.

___ I laugh at inappropriate jokes.

___ I forward emails that degrade women and persons of diverse populations.

___ I fail to confront inappropriate comments.

___ I am embarrassed of my race or ethnicity.

___ I am ashamed of speaking my native tongue.

___ I have assimilated to the environment in which I dwell.

___ I am at-ease in my non-majority group.

___ I am uncomfortable in diverse settings.

___ I have great friends from different races/ethnicities.

___ I pretend that I am having a great experience at college.

___ I wish that I was another race.

___ I despise the people on my residence floor.

___ I had to ignore a racial slur to protect my feelings.

___ I never feel like myself in conversations related to diversity.

___ I wish I could tell someone the reality of my situation without judgment.

> HUMAN RESOURCE BOX:
> How can we help? What do you need? How can we help impact the campus community? How can we effect change? Who have you contacted?

Academic Development: Access to Bias

Chapter 15: Access to Bias

CCA Advisor Directions: Arguably, this is the most important chapter of our entire book because it takes a slight shift from focusing on students to focusing on faculty. This is not an accusation on the part of the authors nor an indictment to the exceptional work the faculty members have done throughout the history of higher education. However, there is cause to argue that not all classroom leaders are trained to facilitate discussions regarding diverse thinking and learning. The student experience has taught us that diversity training is essential to success in the learning environment. Students insist that both students and faculty need diversity education training.

We acknowledge that the responsibility is not solely for the classroom facilitator. The responsibility also falls on the learner. With this in mind, we have attempted to introduce a new concept of teaching and learning that allows both teacher and learner to engage in difficult dialogues away from the margins. It is our intent to create a learning environment conducive to mutual exchange and benefit.

In the following, students and faculty are asked to share their perspectives of the learning experience. This reflection exercise is designed to bring together two perspectives on the classroom experience. This exercise is not meant to criticize the teacher or learner; it is meant to narrow the communication gap between teacher and learner. More importantly, the intent of the exercise is to bring hot topics into the conversation that are often overlooked in the classroom.

In a discussion format, please respond to the following. Here are some ground rules for doing so:

- Be open to dialogue.
- Remove all preconceived notions.
- This discussion is not a debate.
- This discussion should be shared with refreshments.
- Keep in mind that this conversation will help both students and faculty.
- Have fun.

Topics for discussion:

ATTITUDE
1) What was your perception of the class entering week one?
2) What was your expectation of the class entering week one?
3) In what ways were you hoping to be challenged in the classroom?

STRUCTURE
1) Do you feel like this class allowed you to be yourself?
2) Did this class allow open speech and the sharing of opinions?

POLICIES
3) Do you feel the policies were complementary to your teaching/learning style?
4) In what ways did the policies create an imbalance in the classroom?

SERVICES
1) Did you think your services provided access to all students?
2) Do you think classroom discussion created discomfort for students? In what ways?
3) In what ways did your services speak to the diversity mission and vision of the institution?

Academic Development: Diversity Intelligence Rubric

Chapter 15: Developing Diversity Outcomes

CCA Advisor Directions: The following diversity intelligence rubric will serve as a guide for further development and assessment of diversity outcomes. This rubric is essential in the effort to create a more meaningful experience for all students. This tool serves as a moral compass for integrating diversity into the classroom. *We look forward to your assessment of this instrument. Your feedback is welcome.*

Diversity Outcomes	Competency: Attitude	Competency: Structure	Competency: Policies	Competency: Services
Intellectual Deeper understanding of different people, cultures, perspectives	Gain an appreciation of different perceptions of diversity	Understand the importance and value of working with diverse populations in diverse settings	Gain knowledge of how policies impact team cohesiveness and the working environment	Make certain that services do not promote discrimination or alienation
Behavioral Increased comfort with ambiguity and conflict associated with diversity	Develop the ability to be engaged in difficult dialogues effectively	Develop the ability to confront institutional and structural acts of oppression effectively	Generate a work environment conducive to freedom of expression	Identify services that generate unnecessary discomfort and develop a plan for change
Skill-related Practice new ways of framing questions about diversity/globalism	Develop the skills to exchange ideas and be open to new perspectives	Develop knowledge and skills to examine how structure impacts globalism	Develop the skills to examine the development's policies/practices that promote value-based learning	Learn how to develop assessment instruments to evaluate services that lack diversity participation
Affective Examine dispositions, attitudes, and anxieties about diversity and pluralism	Examine the campus climate/unit reaction to diversity initiatives	Develop a greater understanding of how the perspective on diversity impacts team cohesiveness and collaboration	Gain the knowledge and skills to examine why policies that promote social justice are needed	Examine how services connect to the University's mission and vision
Political Examination of the impact of "isms" on society and how social justice structures respond	Create an environment conducive to different perceptions and worldviews	Gain knowledge of how "isms" impact structures, leadership, and decision making	Gain knowledge to examine the impact of "isms" on the planning and execution of decision and policy making	Provide services to support the disruption of "isms"
Descriptive Departmental message via branding	Promote an environment that is welcoming of staff and students of diverse populations	Create opportunities for staff and students of diverse populations to gain access to programs and services	Identify and rewrite policies that promote discrimination and perpetuate stereotypes	Develop marketing strategies to promote services to students and staff of diverse populations

Summary:

1) Did you use the rubric? If so, for how many weeks?

2) Did you find the rubric useful? In what ways?

3) Is there a particular topic you enjoyed the most? Least?

4) What recommendations do you have for us?

References

Agnus, O. Minu, and E. T. Hall. "Proxemics: The Study of Space." *IRWLE* 8, NO. I (2012): 1-7.

Anderson, James A. "Diversity and Global Engagement: Diversity Outcomes." Elon University, Elon, NC, November, 2011.

Astin, Alexander W. *What matters in college: Four critical years revisited*. San Francisco: Jossey-Bass, 1997.

Barkley, Elizabeth F. *Student Engagement Techniques: A handbook for College Faculty*. San Francisco, CA: Jossey-Bass, 2010.

Baxter Magolda, Marcia B., Elizabeth G. Creamer, and Peggy S. Meszaros. "Development and Assessment of Self-authorship: Exploring the Concept Across Cultures." *Stylus* 1 (2010): 300.

Bean, John C. *Engaging Ideas: The professor's guide to integrating writing, critical thinking, and active learning in the classroom*. San Francisco, CA: Jossey-Bass, 2001.

"Benchmark Education: Building Literacy for Life." Benchmark Education Company. Accessed November 20, 2010. http://www.benchmarkeducation.com.

Campbell, David E., and Toni A. Campbell. "The mentoring relationship: Differing perceptions of benefits." *College Student Journal*, 34, (2000): 516-523.

Cohen, Geoffrey L., and Claude M. Steele, "A Barrier of Mistrust: How Negative Stereotypes Affect Cross-Race Mentoring." *Improving academic achievement: Impact of psychological factors on education* (2002): 303-327.

"Community Outreach of Our United Village." Community Asset Mapping. Accessed October 6, 2010. http://www.ouvcommunityoutreach.org

Covey, Stephen. "Time Management Grid." *US Geological Survey: Department of Employee and Organizational Development*. Accessed October 15, 2012. http://www.usgs.gov/humancapital/documents/TimeManagementGrid.pdf.

Earl, Walter R. "Intrusive advising for freshmen." *NACADA journal* 8, no. 2 (1988): 27-33.

Engle, Jennifer and Vincent Tinto. "Moving Beyond Access: College Success for Low-Income, First-Generation Students." *Pell Institute for the Study of Opportunity in Higher Education* (2008).

Evans, Nancy J. *Student Development in College: Theory, Research and Practice*. San Francisco: Jossey-Bass, 2009.

Evans, Nancy, J., Deanna S. Forney, and Florence Guido-DiBrito. "Student Development in College: Theory, research, and practice." *The Journal of General Education* 49.3 (2000): 231-234.

Flavell, John H. "Metacognition and cognitive monitoring: A new era of cognitive-developmental inquiry." *American Psychologist,* 34, no. 10 (1979): 906-911.

Gardner, John N. and Jerome A. Jewler. *Your College Experience: Strategies for Success.* Belmont, CA: Wadsorth/Thompson Learning, 2003.

Gibson, Sharon K. "Being mentored: The experience of women faculty." *Journal of Career Development* 30, no. 3 (2004): 173-188.

Glennon, Robert E., and Dan M. Baxley. "Reduction of Attrition Through Intrusive Advising." *NASPA journal* 22, no 3 (1985): 10-14.

Gordon, Virginia N., Wesley R. Habley, and Thomas J. Grites, eds. *Academic advising: A comprehensive handbook.* John Wiley & Sons, 2011.

Grenny, Joseph, David Maxfield, Ron McMillan, Al Switzer, and Kerry Patterson. *Influencer: The power to change anything.* New York, NY: McGraw-Hill, 2008.

Guiffrida, Douglas A., and Kathryn Z. Douthit. "The Black student experience at predominantly white colleges: Implication for school and college counselors." *Journal of Counseling and Development* 88, no. 3 (2010): 311-318.

Hall, Edward T. *The Hidden Dimension.* New York: Anchor Books, 1990.

Harper, Shaun R. and Sylvia Hurtado. "Nine themes in campus racial climates and implication for institutional transformation." *New Directions for Student Services* 2007, no. 120 (2007): 7-24.

Hawkins, David R. *Power vs. force: The hidden determinants of human behavior.* Carlsbad, California: Hay House Inc., 1995.

Heisserer, D. L., and Phil Parette. "Advising at-risk students in college and university settings." *College Student Journal* 36, no. 1 (2002): 69-83.

Keehner, Julie. "First-year Seminar." Buena Vista University, Storm Lake, IA, September 5, 2005.

Kuyhendall, C. *From Rage to Hope: Strategies for Reclaiming Black & Hispanic Students.* Bloomington, IN: Solution Tree Press, 2004.

Laden, Buerta Vigil. "Socializing and mentoring college students of color: The Puente Project as an exemplary celebratory socialization model." *Peabody Journal of Education* 74, no. 2 (1999): 55-74.

Lee, Wynetta Y. "Striving toward effective retention: The effect of race on mentoring African American students." *Peabody Journal of Education* 74, no. 2 (1999): 27-43.

Lencioni, P. *The Five Dysfunctions of a Team: A Leadership Fable.* San Francisco: Jossey-Bass, 2002.

Livingston, Jennifer A. "Metacognition: An Overview." Lecture on Metacognition, Buffalo University, 1997. Retrieved January 20, 2012, from http://gse.buffalo.edu/fas/shuell/cep564/metacog.htm (accessed August, 2010).

Nash, Robert, J. & Jang, Jennifer, J.J. (2013). The Time Has Come To Create Meaning-Making Centers on College Campuses. *About Campus,* 18 (4), 2-9.

Ogbu, John U. "Collective identity and the burden of "acting White" in black history, community, and education." *The Urban Review* 36, no. 1 (2004): 1-35.

Portman, Joel, Tuyen Trise Bui, Javier Ogaz, and Jesus Trevino. "Microaggressions in the Classroom." Presentation at the University of Denver – Center for Multicultural Excellence, Denver, CO, 2011.

Pritchard, Mary E., and Greagory S. Wilson. "Using emotional and social factors to predict student success." *Journal of college student development* 44, no. 1 (2003): 18-28.

Rosenthal, Kimmo I., and Shelly H. Shinebarger. "In practice: Peer mentors: Helping bridge the advising gap." *About Campus* 15, no. 1 (2010): 24-27.

Shotton, Heather J., E. Star L. Oosahwe, and Rosa Cintron. "Stories of success: Experiences of American Indian students in peer-mentoring retention program." *The Review of Higher Education* 31, no. 1 (2007): 81-107.

Steele, Claude M. *Whistling Vivaldi: How stereotypes affect us and what we ca do.* New York, NY: W.W. Norton & Company, Inc., 2010.

Sue, Derald, Wing, Annie I. Lin, Gina C. Torino, Christina M. Capodilupo, and David P. Rivera. "Racial microaggressions and difficult dialogues on race in the classroom." *Cultural Diversity and Ehtnic Minority Psychology* 15, no. 2 (2009): 183.

Sue, Derald Wing, and David Sue. *Counseling the culturally different: Theory and practice.* Canada: John Wiley & Sons, 2003.

Tinto, Vincent. *Leaving College: Rethinking the causes and cures for student attrition.* Chicago: University of Chicago Press, 1987.

Tinto, Vincent. "Taking retention seriously: Rethinking the first year of college." *NACADA JOURNAL* 19, NO. 2 (1999): 5-9.

Trubowitz, Sidney, and Maureen Picard Robins. *The Good Teacher Mentor: Setting the Standard for Support and Success.* New York: Teachers College Press, 2003.

Upcraft, M. L., John N. Gardner, and Associates. *The Freshman Year Experience: Helping Student Survive and Succeed in College.* San Francisco, CA: Jossey-Bass, Inc., 1989.

Upcraft, M. L., and G. Kramer. "Intrusive advising as discussed in the first-year academic advising: Patterns in the present, pathways to the future." *Academic Advising and Barton College* 1, no. 2 (1995).

Vargas, Robert. "Transformative Knowledge: A Chicano Perspective." *Context Institute.* Last modified Summer 1997. http://www.context.org/iclib/ic17/vargas/.

Author Biography

t. leon Williams, a graduate of Ohio Northern University, B.S.B.A., and The University of Dayton, M.S.E., is currently a doctorate of ministry candidate at Virginia University of Lynchburg.

t. leon williams, founder of Institute for Academic Success and Character Education (iACE), is also a nationally recognized speaker, CAMPUSPEAK, Inc., who has reached more than fifteen thousand students in twenty-five different states.

t. leon williams has served as director of multicultural affairs at Ohio Northern University, Buena Vista University, and Elon University.
Email: leoncharacter.edu@gmail.com

melissa n. jordan graduated with her bachelor's degree from Elon University, where she worked for ten years as a student affairs professional. During her time at Elon, she earned her master's degree from Capella University. She currently works as a student affairs strategist and student success coach. She is devoted to helping students discover their authentic self in pursuit of their academic and social goals.

melissa is a consultant, trainer, and life coach.
Email: melissacharacter.edu@gmail.com

Index

A

Academic Goals, 39-40
Academic Integrity, XX
Academic Playbook, 24
Academic Readiness, 43
Academic Situational Awareness, 98
Academic Space, 77
Academic Wellness, 81
Academic and Social Reflection, 65
Academic and Social Success, 3
Academic Road Trip, 58-59
Academic Spaces, 26
Academic Strategies, 38
Anderson, James, A., 116

B

Barkeley, Elizabeth, F., 110
Bias, 114

C

Character Development, XV
Classroom Preparation, 82
Cluster Groups, XVI-XVII
Covey, Stephen, R., 34
Co-Curricular VIII, IX, XIX, XXV, 9, 11
Communication Log, 12
Consent Form, 6-7
Core Values, XX
Critical Thinking, 101
Curriculum Training Outline, XVIII

D

Diverse Thinking, 112
Diversity Intelligence, 116
Diversity Intelligence Rubric, 116
Doing More by Doing Less, 89

E

Educational Values, 81, 83
Effectiveness, 87-88
Efficiency, 87-88
Emotional Intelligence, 95
Emulating Success, 85
Engaged Learning Differences, 74
Energy Line, 19-20
Epistemology, 73
Erasing Doubt, 109

F

Finish Line, 108
Flavell, John, .H., 46

G

Gardner, John, .N., VIII
Goals, 36-38

H

Hall, Edward, T., 77
Headlines, 70

I

Identity Development, 101
Interpersonal, 73
Intrapersonal, 73
Introduction Letter, 10
Intrusive Advising, IX, XIX

J

Journey Walk, 80

L

Learning, 48
Learning Committee, 11
Learning Environment, 27
Learning Outcomes, 83

M

Managing Goals, 36-37
Meaning-making, 68
Meaningful Relationships, 77
Mentoring Philosophy, XV
Metacognition, 46-47

Metamemory, 46
Metacomprehension, 46
Microaggressions, 103
Microinsults, 103
Mid-term Preparation, 60
    Social, 61-62
    Physical, 61-62
    Emotional, 61-62
    Intellectual, 61-62
    Spiritual, 61-62
    Occupational, 61-62

Mumford, Michael, D., 46
Mind-mapping, 55

N

Nash, Robert, 68

P

Pairings, XII
Parents/Guardians, IV
Personal Asset Mapping, 41-42
Personal Contract, 21
Personal Development, 23
Personal Value Assessment, 51
Personal Journal, 50
Personal Space, 77
Personal Talk Journal, 16
Public Space, 77

R

Reading and Writing Skills, 82
Reading the Environment, 53
Relationships, 1

S

Self-Authorship, 72-73
Self-care, 23
Self-image, 4
Self-regulation, 46
Social Involvement, 82
Social Situational Awareness, 96
Social Space, 77
Stereotype threat, 105
Strategies for Academic and Social Success, 6
Student Advocate, XI, XV, 9, 10, 12, 13, 14
    Student Advocate Mentoring
    Philosophy, XV
    Student Advocate Profile, XVI
    Student Advocate Training, XVII, XVIII

Student Intelligence, 72
Student Learning Outcomes, XXV
Students of Diverse Populations, XIX
Student Profile Form, 8-9
Study Habits, 17, 82-83
Steele, Claude, 105
Support, X
Support Staff, 76

T

Test Preparation, 82
Theoretical Framework, IX
Time Management, 31-32, 82
    Time Management Matrix, 33-34
Time Pie, 28
Time Waster, 30
Tinto, Vincent, X
Transferrable Skills, 63
Transformative Knowledge, 91
Transformative Experience, 103

U

Upcraft, M.L., VIII, IX

V

Value Inventory, 17
Vargas, Robert, 103

Made in the USA
Monee, IL
09 July 2022